Mediterranean Air Fryer Cookbook for Beginners

2000 Days of Effortless, Budget-Friendly, and Family-Friendly Air Fryer Recipes | Hassle-Free Meal Guide

Lagnol Ylington

Table of Contents

INTRODUCTION

What Is The Mediterranean Diet And Its Advantages?

The Mediterranean Diet is a renowned and highly regarded dietary pattern that has gained popularity worldwide due to its numerous health benefits and delicious culinary traditions. It is not just a diet but a way of life followed by people in the Mediterranean region, which includes countries like Greece, Italy, Spain, and Southern France. This dietary regimen is based on the traditional eating habits of these regions and has been associated with various advantages for overall well-being.

- Heart Health: One of the primary advantages of the Mediterranean Diet is its positive impact on heart health. It's rich in heart-healthy monounsaturated fats, primarily from olive oil. These fats help lower LDL (bad) cholesterol levels while maintaining HDL (good) cholesterol levels. Additionally, the diet is low in saturated fats and processed foods, reducing the risk of heart diseases.

- Weight Management: The Mediterranean Diet focuses on whole, unprocessed foods, including an abundance of fruits, vegetables, whole grains, and lean proteins. This promotes satiety and makes it easier for individuals to manage their weight. It's not a restrictive diet but emphasizes portion control and balanced nutrition.

- Reduced Risk of Chronic Diseases: Studies have shown that the

Mediterranean Diet is associated with a lower risk of chronic diseases like type 2 diabetes, certain cancers, and neurodegenerative conditions such as Alzheimer's disease. The high intake of antioxidants, fiber, and anti-inflammatory foods in this diet contributes to these health benefits.

- Longevity: Mediterranean countries are often associated with longer lifespans, and the Mediterranean Diet may be a contributing factor. It includes foods rich in antioxidants, such as fresh fruits, vegetables, and red wine (in moderation), which have been linked to increased longevity.

- Improved Cognitive Function: The diet is linked to better cognitive function and a reduced risk of cognitive decline. The inclusion of fish, particularly fatty fish like salmon and mackerel, as well as nuts and olive oil, provides essential nutrients for brain health.

- Lower Risk of Depression: The Mediterranean Diet's emphasis on whole, nutrient-dense foods, including omega-3 fatty acids from fish, can positively impact mental health. Studies suggest a lower risk of depression and a better overall mood among those who follow this diet.

- Diverse and Enjoyable: Perhaps one of the most appealing aspects of the Mediterranean Diet is that it is delicious and highly adaptable. It encourages a wide variety of flavorful foods, making it more sustainable and enjoyable for those who follow it.

In summary, the Mediterranean Diet is not just a fad but a holistic approach to nutrition and well-being. Its advantages range from improved heart health and weight management to a reduced risk of chronic diseases, enhanced cognitive function, and even potential longevity. This dietary pattern is not only a recipe for good health but also a recipe for savoring the pleasures of life through delicious and nutritious food. A Mediterranean Air Fryer Cookbook can be a great way to enjoy the benefits of this diet while adding a modern twist to traditional recipes.

How Can Traditional Mediterranean Recipes Be Adapted For Air Frying?

Adapting traditional Mediterranean recipes for air frying is an innovative approach that combines the rich flavors of this cuisine with the convenience and health benefits of air frying. The Mediterranean diet is renowned for its focus on fresh, wholesome ingredients like olive oil, vegetables, grains, and lean proteins. When transitioning these recipes to the air fryer, there are several key considerations to keep in mind:

- Use Less Oil: One of the primary advantages of air frying is that it significantly reduces the need for oil while achieving a similar crispy texture. In traditional Mediterranean recipes, olive oil is often a key ingredient. When air frying, you can still use olive oil, but in smaller quantities. Alternatively, you can employ olive oil spray to lightly coat your ingredients.

- Opt for Healthier Coatings: Instead of traditional breading or batter, use alternatives like panko breadcrumbs or crushed nuts for coating. These options add a crunchy texture and nutty flavor without the need for excessive oil.

- Adjust Temperatures and Cooking Times: Air fryers cook at high temperatures and circulate hot air around the food to create a crispy exterior. For Mediterranean dishes, it's essential to adjust cooking times and temperatures to ensure the ingredients cook through while retaining their moisture and tenderness. Experimentation may be necessary to find

the perfect settings for specific recipes.

- Maximize Seasonings: Mediterranean cuisine relies heavily on herbs and spices for flavor. In air frying, these seasonings become even more prominent due to the reduced use of oil. Fresh herbs like rosemary, thyme, and oregano can be added directly to your air-fried dishes, enhancing the overall taste.

- Pay Attention to Texture: Air frying provides a unique texture to dishes, and this can either complement or contrast with traditional Mediterranean recipes. For instance, falafel can become extra crunchy in an air fryer, while vegetables can retain more of their natural crispness. Ensure the texture aligns with your desired outcome.

- Utilize the Versatility: Air fryers are versatile appliances, capable of baking, grilling, roasting, and more. Adapt your Mediterranean recipes to these different functions for various results. For example, roast a whole fish with Mediterranean seasonings for a delightful twist on the classic baked fish.

- Monitor Doneness: Keep a close eye on your dishes as they cook in the air fryer, as cooking times can vary. Use a meat thermometer for proteins to ensure they reach safe internal temperatures.

Incorporating these adaptations into your traditional Mediterranean recipes for the air fryer can lead to healthier and equally delicious dishes. It allows you to enjoy the flavors of the Mediterranean diet with the added benefits of reduced oil and quicker cooking times. Ultimately, experimenting and fine-tuning the process will help you achieve the perfect balance of taste, texture, and healthfulness in your air-fried Mediterranean dishes.

What Is The Versatility Of Mediterranean Cooking With An Air Fryer?

The versatility of Mediterranean cooking with an air fryer is truly remarkable, as it combines the traditional and healthy aspects of Mediterranean cuisine with the modern convenience and efficiency of air frying. This culinary fusion not only makes it easier to prepare Mediterranean dishes but also enhances their flavors and nutritional value.

- Healthier Cooking: Mediterranean cuisine is renowned for its use of fresh ingredients, olive oil, and lean proteins. When you use an air fryer, you can maintain the heart-healthy qualities of this diet. The air fryer uses hot air circulation to cook food, reducing the need for excessive oil. This method preserves the flavors and textures of Mediterranean dishes while keeping them low in saturated fats.

- Retained Nutrients: The Mediterranean diet is rich in fruits, vegetables, and whole grains, providing a wide range of essential nutrients. When using an air fryer, the rapid cooking process preserves the

nutrients in these ingredients. Vegetables stay crisp and colorful, and seafood remains moist and tender. This means you can enjoy all the health benefits of Mediterranean ingredients without overcooking or losing their nutritional value.

- Flavor Enhancement: The air fryer's ability to achieve a crispy texture and beautiful golden-brown finish without deep-frying is a game-changer for Mediterranean cooking. Whether it's falafel, crispy pita chips, or even baklava, the air fryer brings out the flavors and textures that make Mediterranean cuisine so appealing.

- Wide Range of Dishes: The Mediterranean diet offers a wide variety of dishes, from Greek salads and stuffed grape leaves to shawarma and kebabs. With an air fryer, you can prepare all these dishes with ease. The appliance's versatility allows you to roast, bake, grill, and even dehydrate ingredients, giving you endless options for creating Mediterranean-inspired meals.

- Time Efficiency: Mediterranean cooking often involves marinating and slow roasting. An air fryer significantly reduces cooking time, allowing you to whip up your favorite Mediterranean dishes in a fraction of the time. This is especially convenient for busy individuals and families who want to enjoy healthy, homemade meals without the lengthy preparation.

In conclusion, the versatility of Mediterranean cooking with an air fryer not only simplifies the preparation of these delicious and nutritious dishes but also enhances their taste and nutritional value. Whether you're a fan of Greek, Italian, or Middle Eastern cuisine, the air fryer can become an indispensable tool in your kitchen, making it easier than ever to enjoy the diverse and wholesome flavors of the Mediterranean diet.

What Are The Health Benefits Of Following A Mediterranean Air Frying Diet?

Following a Mediterranean air frying diet can offer a plethora of health benefits, making it a smart and delicious choice for those looking to maintain or improve their overall well-being. The Mediterranean diet, characterized by its emphasis on fresh, whole foods, has long been associated with a reduced risk of chronic diseases and an increased life expectancy. When combined with the cooking method of air frying, which uses hot air to cook food with little to no oil, the benefits are further enhanced. Here's an in-depth look at the health advantages of adopting a Mediterranean air frying diet:

- Heart Health: The Mediterranean diet is renowned for its heart-healthy qualities. It's rich in monounsaturated fats from sources like olive oil, which can help lower bad cholesterol levels. When air frying, you can use minimal oil or none at all, reducing saturated and trans fats, which are detrimental to heart health. The result is a diet that supports healthy blood pressure and reduces the risk of heart disease.

- Weight Management: Air frying allows you to enjoy the taste and texture of traditionally fried foods with significantly fewer calories and fat. This can aid in weight management by reducing overall calorie intake while still providing satisfying, crispy meals. The Mediterranean diet's focus on lean proteins, whole grains, and fresh produce further contributes to maintaining a healthy weight.

- Diabetes Management: The Mediterranean diet is rich in fiber, which helps regulate blood sugar levels. Air frying enables you to enjoy carbohydrates like sweet potatoes or whole grains with a lower glycemic index due to the reduced oil content. This can be particularly beneficial for individuals with diabetes or those at risk of developing the condition.

- Antioxidant-Rich Foods: The Mediterranean diet includes a wide variety of fruits and vegetables, which are rich in antioxidants. Air frying preserves the nutrient content of these foods better than deep frying, ensuring you get the maximum health benefits from them. Antioxidants help combat free radicals and reduce the risk of chronic diseases.

- Reduced Inflammation: The Mediterranean diet's emphasis on foods like fish, nuts, and olive oil provides essential omega-3 fatty acids and polyphenols, which have anti-inflammatory properties. Air frying maintains the integrity of these ingredients, contributing to the diet's anti-inflammatory benefits.

- Digestive Health: With its fiber-rich foods, the Mediterranean diet supports a healthy digestive system. Air frying doesn't cause the excessive oil that can lead to digestive discomfort, making it a gentle cooking method for those with sensitive stomachs.

- Longevity: Studies have shown that the Mediterranean diet is associated with increased life expectancy. The combination of nutrient-rich foods, reduced saturated fats, and preserved antioxidants in an air frying method all contribute to the potential for a longer, healthier life.

In conclusion, a Mediterranean air frying diet offers a range of health benefits, including improved heart health, weight management, diabetes control, antioxidant intake, reduced inflammation, enhanced digestive health, and the potential for a longer life. By embracing this dietary approach, you can savor flavorful, satisfying dishes while supporting your overall well-being.

What Are Some Common Troubleshooting Issues And Solutions When Air Frying?

Air frying Mediterranean dishes can be a delightful and healthy way to enjoy the rich flavors of this cuisine. However, like any cooking method, air frying can come with its share of troubleshooting issues. Here are some common problems that may arise when air frying Mediterranean dishes, along with their solutions:

- Uneven Cooking: One of the primary issues in air frying is uneven cooking. Some parts of your dish may be overcooked while others are undercooked. To address this, ensure you spread the ingredients evenly in the air fryer basket and avoid overcrowding, as crowded baskets can hinder the circulation of hot air. You can also shake or flip the ingredients midway through the cooking process to promote even cooking.

- Food Sticking to the Basket: Foods like falafel, fritters, or coated items can stick to the air fryer basket. To prevent this, lightly grease the basket or use parchment paper or silicone mats to line it. This not only prevents sticking but also makes cleanup easier.

- Dry or Overcooked Food: Mediterranean dishes often feature lean proteins

and vegetables, which can become dry when air-fried for too long. To avoid this, pay attention to cooking times and temperatures. Use a food thermometer to ensure the food is cooked to the right internal temperature without overcooking it. You can also marinate or coat your ingredients with a little olive oil to help retain moisture.

- Burnt Seasonings: The high heat in the air fryer can cause seasonings like herbs and spices to burn. To prevent this, add herbs and spices towards the end of the cooking process or use larger pieces of fresh herbs as a garnish after cooking. This will preserve their flavor and prevent them from turning bitter.

- Soggy Coatings: When making crispy Mediterranean favorites like eggplant Parmesan or fried calamari, the coating can become soggy if not properly air fried.

To achieve a crispy texture, make sure to preheat your air fryer, evenly coat the food with a thin layer of oil or cooking spray, and cook in batches to prevent overcrowding.

- Food Sticking Together: If you're cooking items like meatballs or kebabs, they can stick together during air frying. To prevent this, give them enough space in the basket and consider using skewers or racks to keep them separated. This will ensure that they cook evenly without sticking.

- Overwhelming Smoke: Some Mediterranean recipes involve oil or marinades that can create smoke in the air fryer. To mitigate this, use oils with higher smoke points like grapeseed or avocado oil. Additionally, consider using a drip tray or aluminum foil to catch any drippings that could cause smoke.

By understanding and addressing these common troubleshooting issues, you can enjoy delicious Mediterranean dishes with your air fryer while maintaining the authentic flavors and textures of this cuisine. Experimenting with different techniques and making adjustments as needed will help you achieve the perfect results with your air fryer and Mediterranean recipes.

Chapter 1: Breakfast and Brunch

Frittata

Prep Time: 15 Mins   Cook Time: 20 Mins   Serves: 2

Ingredients:

- cooking spray
- ¼ pound breakfast sausage, fully cooked and crumbled
- 4 large eggs, lightly beaten
- ½ cup shredded Cheddar-Monterey Jack cheese blend
- 2 tablespoons red bell pepper, diced
- 1 green onion, chopped
- 1 pinch cayenne pepper (Optional)

Directions:

1. Preheat an air fryer to 360 degrees F. Spray a nonstick 6x2-inch cake pan with cooking spray.
2. Combine sausage, eggs, cheese, bell pepper, green onion, and cayenne pepper in a large bowl; mix well to combine.
3. Pour egg mixture into the prepared cake pan.
4. Cook in the preheated air fryer until frittata is set, 18 to 20 minutes.

Nutritional Value (Amount per Serving):

Calories: 289; Fat: 19.71; Carb: 12.28; Protein: 16.16

Vegetable Medley

Prep Time: 15 Mins   Cook Time: 10 Mins   Serves: 4

Ingredients:

- ½ small eggplant, cut into 1/4-inch thick slices and wedged (2 cups)
- 1 small zucchini, cut into 1/4-inch slices (1 1/4 cups)
- 1 small summer squash, cut into 1/4-inch slices (1 cup)
- 1 cup shiitake mushrooms, stemmed and sliced
- 1 cup whole grape tomatoes
- 2 tablespoon olive oil
- 2 cloves garlic, minced
- ½ teaspoon dried oregano
- ½ teaspoon kosher salt
- 1 teaspoon lemon zest

Directions:

1. In a large bowl, combine eggplant, zucchini, summer squash, mushrooms, tomatoes, olive oil, garlic, oregano, and salt. Working in batches if necessary, cook vegetables in an even layer at 360°F for 10 minutes,

stirring halfway through, until tender and edges are golden brown. Keep cooked vegetables warm in a 200°F oven while cooking the rest. Sprinkle with lemon zest before serving.

Nutritional Value (Amount per Serving):

Calories: 109; Fat: 6.97; Carb: 12.35; Protein: 1.23

Nutrisystem Flatbread

Prep Time: 10 Mins   Cook Time: 15 Mins   Serves: 4

Ingredients:

- 1 package Nutrisystem Mediterranean Flatbread

Directions:

1. Preheat air fryer to 350°F.
2. Place Mediterranean Flatbread into the air fryer and cook for 8 minutes, or until hot.
3. Please note that all air fryers cook differently. Before trying any recipe, always refer to the manufacturer safety instructions provided with your specific air fryer.

Nutritional Value (Amount per Serving):

Calories: 97; Fat: 5.95; Carb: 11.02; Protein: 0.67

Chickpea Bowl

Prep Time: 10 Mins   Cook Time: 15 Mins   Serves: 4

Ingredients:

- 1 can chickpeas
- 1 tbsp avocado oil
- Salt and pepper
- 1 tsp garlic powder
- 1 cucumber, diced
- ½ onion (red or yellow), diced
- ½ cup cherry tomatoes
- ½ cup kale or spinach
- 1/8 cup fresh basil, chopped
- 1/2 lemon

Directions:

1. Drain and rinse chickpeas and dry with a paper towel. Place in a bowl with ½ tbsp oil, ½ tsp garlic powder, and lightly add salt and pepper. Toss to coat and place into the air fryer. Bake at 375 degrees for 10 minutes, shake, and cook for another 5 minutes until crispy.
2. Add the diced cucumber, onion, kale, and tomatoes to a bowl with ½ tbsp oil, ½ tsp garlic powder and small amount of salt and pepper. Add about half of the basil and mix.

3. Place the vegetables and chickpeas together in a bowl and serve with remaining basil and freshly squeezed lemon juice if desired. Top with balsamic vinaigrette dressing or tzatziki sauce.

Nutritional Value (Amount per Serving):

Calories: 149; Fat: 5.45; Carb: 20.91; Protein: 5.52

Air Fryer Cherry Tomatoes

Prep Time: 5 Mins   Cook Time: 15 Mins   Serves: 2

Ingredients:

- 2 cups cherry tomatoes
- 2 teaspoon olive oil
- ¼ teaspoon salt
- ¼ teaspoon dried oregano

Directions:

1. Wash and dry your tomatoes.
2. Next, slice each in half lengthwise and add to a medium bowl.
3. Add the oil, salt, and oregano and stir or toss to combine.
4. Add the tomatoes into the air fryer basket in a single layer, skin side down.
5. Cook at 400 degrees F for 10 minutes, checking around the 8 minute mark for doneness.

Nutritional Value (Amount per Serving):

Calories: 45; Fat: 4.52; Carb: ; Protein: 0.1

Air Fryer Flatbread Pizza

Prep Time: 5 Mins   Cook Time: 9 Mins   Serves: 1

Ingredients:

- 1 Flatbread
- 2 tablespoons tomato sauce
- ¼ teaspoon dried oregano
- A handful of mozzarella cheese
- Few leaves of fresh basil

Directions:

1. Take the flatbread and make sure it will fit in your air fryer basket. If not, slice it with a knife or pizza cutter.
2. Spread tomato sauce onto the flatbread.
3. Sprinkle dried oregano onto the tomato sauce.
4. Add as much mozzarella cheese as you like.
5. Place in the air fryer basket and cook at 390 degrees F for 4 minutes, checking at the 3 minute mark for doneness.
6. Remove from the air fryer, slice if desired, and top with fresh basil leaves.

Nutritional Value (Amount per Serving):

Calories: 404; Fat: 21.85; Carb: ; Protein: 18.37

Air Fryer Egg Bites

Prep Time: 6 Mins   Cook Time: 16 Mins   Serves: 6

Ingredients:

- 5 eggs
- 1 cup chopped spinach
- 1/3 cup diced red pepper
- ¼ cup crumbled goat cheese
- 3 tablespoons unsweetened almond milk
- salt and pepper to taste

Directions:

1. First, preheat your air fryer. If your air fryer has a preheating option you can preheat your air fryer. If you don't have that option, you can run the machine at 300 degrees F for 2-5 minutes. Leave the machine running for about 3 minutes for smaller air fryers. Leave the machine running for about 5 minutes for larger air fryers.
2. In a large mixing bowl, crack 5 eggs and add in chopped spinach, diced red pepper, crumbled goat cheese, unsweetened almond milk and salt and pepper to taste.
3. Whisk all of the ingredients together.
4. Grab 6 silicone cups. I like to spray them with a little avocado oil. It's not necessary, but I do it sometimes just to make sure nothing sticks.
5. Evenly distribute the egg mixture into each cup, filling ¾ of the way.
6. Place the filled silicone cups into the air fryer. Air fry at 300 degrees F for 8-10 minutes.
7. Allow the egg bites to cool completely before removing them from the silicone cups.

Nutritional Value (Amount per Serving):

Calories: 123; Fat: 8.6; Carb: 2.77; Protein: 8.22

Air-Fryer Breakfast Bowl

Prep Time: 15 Mins   Cook Time: 30 Mins   Serves: 4

Ingredients:

- 1 ½ teaspoons canola oil
- 2 ½ tablespoons lower-sodium taco seasoning, divided
- 1 cup thinly sliced multi-coloured baby peppers

- 1 cup multi-coloured cherry tomatoes
- ½ cup thinly sliced scallions, whites and greens separated
- 4 (6 inch) whole-wheat flour tortillas
- ¾ cup finely shredded pepper Jack cheese
- 8 large eggs, divided
- Pinch of salt
- Cilantro sprigs, thinly sliced red onion and/or lime wedges for garnish

Directions:

1. Line the basket of an air fryer with foil. Whisk oil and 1 tablespoon taco seasoning together in a medium bowl. Add peppers, tomatoes and scallion whites; toss to coat. Place on the foil in the air-fryer basket. Cook at 400°F until the vegetables are slightly tender and lightly browned, about 8 minutes. Remove by grasping the foil and lifting from the basket, then gather the foil around the vegetables to form a pouch. Set aside to keep warm.
2. Preheat the air fryer to 320°F for 10 minutes. Meanwhile, place each tortilla in a 4-inch-diameter shallow ramekin or heatproof bowl, pressing the tortilla to fit it into the bottom. Sprinkle each tortilla with 3 tablespoons shredded cheese and crack 2 eggs on top. Sprinkle each ramekin evenly with salt and the remaining 1 1/2 tablespoons taco seasoning.
3. Once the air fryer is preheated, carefully line the basket with a large piece of foil that will extend beyond the ramekins to act as handles later. Place the ramekins on the foil, folding excess foil inside the basket, out of the way. Cook, in batches as needed, until the egg whites are set and yolks are still runny, about 10 minutes. Carefully grasp the foil handles to lift the hot ramekins out of the basket.
4. To serve, spoon 1/4 cup of the vegetables over each ramekin. Garnish with scallion greens, cilantro, red onion and/or lime wedges, if desired.

Nutritional Value (Amount per Serving):

Calories: 415; Fat: 26.69; Carb: 21.68; Protein: 21.89

Air Fryer Breakfast Banana Split

Prep Time: 2 Mins   Cook Time: 7 Mins   Serves: 1

Ingredients:

- 1 medium ripe banana
- 2 teaspoons pure maple syrup
- ground cinnamon
- 1/2 cup non-fat Greek yogurt
- 2 tablespoons pecan halves, chopped

- optional: colored sprinkles and cherry, for topping

Directions:

1. Slice the banana lengthwise, 3/4 of the way through on the side of the banana so it doesn't roll in the air fryer and open the skin and banana slightly.
2. Top with cinnamon and air fry 400°F 5 to 6 minutes, until soft.
3. Meanwhile in a small bowl, combine 1 teaspoon syrup with the yogurt.
4. When the banana is ready, top with yogurt, sprinkle with more cinnamon and the nuts and drizzle with the remaining 1 teaspoon maple syrup.
5. Optional, top with colored sprinkles and a cherry on top.

Nutritional Value (Amount per Serving):

Calories: 452; Fat: 16.83; Carb: 58.36; Protein: 23.28

Air Fryer Egg Cabbage Pancake With Mediterranean Dip

Prep Time: 10 Mins   Cook Time: 30 Mins   Serves: 8

Ingredients:

- 1 big Onion (sliced in small pieces)
- 1 big Potato (sliced in small pieces)
- 1 big Green bell peppers (sliced in small pieces)
- 1 medium Carrot (sliced in small pieces)
- 1/2 Cabbage (sliced in small pieces)
- 2 Eggs
- 1/2 cup Spring onion
- 1/2 cup all-purpose flour
- Salt to taste
- Olive oil for air frying

Directions:

1. Cut the potatoes into thin pieces and then in a bowl add water and put the potato pieces in that till you use them or completely cut other vegetables. When all ingredients are ready just drain out the water and pat dry the potato pieces.
2. Wash all the vegetables then cut all the vegetables like potato, onion, cabbage, bell peppers, and carrot in fine pieces.
3. Add all the finely sliced vegetables in a bowl and add all-purpose flour, salt to taste, and black pepper powder.
4. Now crack and add 2 eggs into a bowl.
5. Add chopped spring onion to this.
6. Mix everything nicely. If you feel the mixture is dry just add a little water and mix properly into a smooth mixture. It should not be very runny. Keep

aside for 10 minutes when mixed properly.

7. Now let's prepare the Mediterranean dip. For that in a small bowl add all the chopped garlic, red bell pepper, jalapeno, red chili flakes, paprika, and salt to taste.
8. Now heat olive oil in a small pan for tempering. Once the oil has reached the smoking point add the hot oil to the mixture. Mix well.
9. Now add chopped coriander leaves and mix well.
10. Take a plate and spread Greek yogurt or hung curd with a spoon.
11. Now add the mixture we prepared for the dip. The dip is ready to keep aside.
12. Put parchment paper in the air fryer basket and add some vegetable pancake mixture to the paper.
13. Now make a hole or space in the middle.
14. Add an egg yolk in the middle.
15. Now spray or brush some oil on the vegetable egg pancake.
16. Now air fry them at 380 degrees F for 15 minutes. Then check and flip the pancake once you see golden brown and crisp on the top side.
17. Now again air fry at 380 degrees F for 6 to 8 minutes.
18. Once golden and crisp take it out with the help of a spatula. You can air fry 2 vegetable eggs pancake according to your air fryer size. Take out and serve hot.
19. Serve them hot with the Mediterranean dip we prepared. Enjoy.

Nutritional Value (Amount per Serving):

Calories: 126; Fat: 4.29; Carb: 17.29; Protein: 4.51

Stuffed Peppers

Prep Time: 15 Mins   Cook Time: 40 Mins   Serves: 4

Ingredients:

- 4 bell pepper
- 1 cup cooked quinoa
- 1 cup cooked and seasoned chicken (can be leftovers from other dishes)
- 1/2 cup diced tomatoes
- 1/4 cup diced red onion
- 1/4 cup diced cucumber
- 1/4 cup crumbled feta cheese
- 2 tablespoons olive oil
- 1 teaspoon dried oregano
- Salt and pepper to taste
- Fresh parsley or mint leaves for garnish

Directions:

1. Preheat your air fryer to 370°F.
2. Cut the tops off the bell peppers, remove the seeds and membranes, and set them aside.
3. In a large bowl, combine the cooked quinoa or couscous, seasoned ground meat, diced tomatoes, diced red onion, diced cucumber, crumbled feta cheese, olive oil, dried oregano, salt, and pepper. Mix well.
4. Stuff the hollowed-out bell peppers with the mixture.
5. Place the stuffed peppers in the air fryer basket. Depending on the size of your air fryer, you may need to cook them in batches. Air fry at 370°F for about 20-25 minutes until the peppers are tender and slightly charred on the outside.
6. Remove the stuffed peppers from the air fryer, garnish with fresh parsley or mint leaves, and serve hot.

Nutritional Value (Amount per Serving):

Calories: 303; Fat: 21.32; Carb: 18.24; Protein: 10.95

Breakfast Pita Pockets

Prep Time: 15 Mins   Cook Time: 25 Mins   Serves: 2

Ingredients:

- 2 whole-wheat pita pockets
- 4 large eggs
- 1/4 cup crumbled feta cheese
- 1/2 cup diced tomatoes
- 1/4 cup diced cucumber
- 1/4 cup diced red bell pepper
- 1/4 cup diced red onion
- 1/4 cup chopped fresh parsley
- 1/4 cup olive oil
- 1 tablespoon lemon juice
- 1 teaspoon dried oregano
- Salt and pepper to taste

Directions:

1. Preheat your air fryer to 350°F beforehand.
2. Slice the whole-wheat pita pockets in half to create two pockets. Carefully open each pocket to create space for the filling.
3. In a bowl, whisk the eggs and add a pinch of salt and pepper (to taste).
4. Pour the eggs mix into the air fryer basket. Cook at 350°F for 5-7 minutes or until the eggs are set. Once cooked, break the eggs into smaller pieces.
5. In another bowl, combine the diced tomatoes, cucumber, red bell pepper, red onion, and chopped fresh parsley.
6. In another bowl, make the dressing by whisking together the olive oil, lemon juice, dried oregano, and a pinch of salt.
7. Stuff the cooked eggs, salad mixture, and crumbled feta cheese into each pita pocket.

8. Drizzle the dressing over the fillings in each pita pocket.

9. Serve the pita pockets while warm.

Nutritional Value (Amount per Serving):

Calories: 503; Fat: 41.01; Carb: 24.51; Protein: 12.23

Air Fryer Breakfast Potatoes

Prep Time: 10 Mins   Cook Time: 28 Mins   Serves: 4

Ingredients:

- 2 medium bell peppers any color combination
- 2 large russet potatoes
- 1 teaspoon garlic powder
- 1 teaspoon onion powder
- 1/2 teaspoon salt
- 1/2 teaspoon pepper
- 1 tablespoon parsley
- 1/2 teaspoon chili powder
- 1 tablespoon olive oil

Directions:

1. Remove the seeds from the peppers, and then rinse and chop into 1/4"-1/2" pieces. Set them aside.
2. Scrub the potatoes well under cold water.
3. Dice the potatoes into 1/4"-1/2" pieces and then add them to a mixing bowl.
4. Preheat the Air fryer to 400°F. This should take about 5 minutes.
5. Add the peppers to the diced potatoes and mix.
6. Mix all the spices together in a small bowl.
7. Add the spices to the potatoes and toss to coat.
8. Drizzle the potatoes and peppers with olive oil and toss until they are evenly coated.
9. Add the potatoes to the air fryer basket and then shake the basket to force the potatoes and peppers to settle.
10. Air fry at 400°F for 18 minutes, shake the air fryer basket every 3-4 minutes.
11. Once the potatoes and peppers are done, remove them and let them cool for a couple of minutes.

Nutritional Value (Amount per Serving):

Calories: 193; Fat: 3.65; Carb: 37.27; Protein: 4.78

Chapter 2: Vegetarian Mains

Air-Fryer Root Veg With Garlic and Herbs

Prep Time: 10 Mins   Cook Time: 35 Mins   Serves: 4

Ingredients:

- 640 g root veg , such as carrot, butternut squash, parsnip, swede
- olive oil
- 4 cloves of garlic
- 2 sprigs of fresh rosemary
- red wine vinegar

Directions:

1. Roughly chop the root veg into 2cm chunks (there's no need to peel it).
2. Place in a large bowl with 1 tablespoon of olive oil and a pinch of sea salt and black pepper. Toss together until well coated.
3. Place the veg in the air-fryer and cook for 25 minutes, turning the veg over or shaking the basket every 10 minutes.
4. Peel and slice the garlic, pick and roughly chop the rosemary
5. Add the garlic, rosemary and a splash of red wine vinegar to the air-fryer and toss together with the veg, then cook for a final 10 minutes, or until cooked through and golden.

Nutritional Value (Amount per Serving):

Calories: 174; Fat: 4.44; Carb: 32.93; Protein: 1.82

Brussels Sprouts

Prep Time: 5 Mins   Cook Time: 18 Mins   Serves: 6

Ingredients:

- 1 pound Brussels sprouts, halved
- 1 tablespoon olive oil
- 1 teaspoon kosher salt
- 1 teaspoon white pepper
- 1/4 cup garlic chili paste
- 1 tablespoon honey
- 2 tablespoons water
- Sesame seeds, for garnish

Directions:

1. Gather the ingredients.
2. In a large bowl, toss the Brussels sprouts with olive oil, salt, and white pepper until the sprouts are nicely coated.
3. Place the Brussels sprouts into the basket of your air fryer—they do not need to be in 1 layer, but if you'd like them extra crispy, place them in 1 layer and cook them in batches. Turn your air fryer to 390°F and cook for 9 minutes. Once the time is up, shake the basket and fry for an additional 9 minutes.

4. Whisk together the garlic chili paste, honey, and 2 tablespoons of water in a small bowl. Place the bowl in the microwave and heat, covered, for 1 minute or until the sauce is hot.
5. Once the Brussels sprouts are done, place them in a large bowl and toss them with the sauce while hot.
6. Sprinkle with sesame seeds. Serve immediately for the crispiest results.
7. Enjoy!

Nutritional Value (Amount per Serving):

Calories: 81; Fat: 3.33; Carb: 11.95; Protein: 3.24

Falafel

Prep Time: 10 Mins   Cook Time: 14 Mins   Serves: 6

Ingredients:

For The Tahini Sauce:
- 1/2 cup tahini
- 1/4 cup Greek yogurt
- 1/2 lemon, juice only
- 2 tablespoons olive oil
- 1/4 to 1/2 cup hot water

For The Falafel:
- 2 (15-ounce) cans chickpeas, rinsed and drained
- 1/4 cup fresh parsley
- 1/4 cup cilantro
- 2 cloves garlic
- 1 large shallot, chopped
- 3 tablespoons all-purpose flour
- 2 tablespoons sesame seeds
- 2 teaspoons ground cumin
- 1 teaspoon paprika
- 1/2 lemon, juice only
- 1 teaspoon salt
- Spray olive oil, for cooking

For Serving:
- 6 pita breads
- Fresh lettuce
- 1 large tomato, sliced thinly
- 1/2 red onion, sliced thinly
- 1 cucumber, sliced thinly

Directions:

1. Make the tahini sauce: In a medium bowl, stir together tahini, yogurt, lemon juice, and olive oil. The mixture will be very thick to start. Thin it out with hot water until it's easily spreadable. You'll have to slowly add 1/4 to 1/2 cup of hot water to get it to the right consistency
2. Make the falafel mixture: In the bowl of a food processor, add the chickpeas, parsley, cilantro, garlic, shallot, flour, sesame seeds, cumin, paprika, lemon, and salt. Pulse until mixture comes together in a rough paste. It shouldn't be completely smooth.
3. Shape the falafel mixture into tablespoon-sized discs, about 1-inch in diameter. Repeat until you use all the falafel mixture. You should get 25 to 30 falafel discs.
4. Air fry the falafel: Spray the basket for your air fryer with some nonstick

olive oil. Add as many falafel discs into the basket as you can without them touching and spray them with olive oil very lightly. Air fry the falafel at 350°F for 8 minutes. Flip and fry for another 6 minutes on the second side.

5. Repeat until you've cooked all the falafel.
6. Serve the falafel: Serve the falafel in warm pita. Serve with tahini yogurt sauce and any toppings you like!
7. Leftover falafel will store great in the fridge for 5 to 6 days or you can freeze the falafel for longer storage. Reheat falafel in a 350°F oven for 10 to 12 minutes until warmed through.

Nutritional Value (Amount per Serving):

Calories: 419; Fat: 22.15; Carb: 44.64; Protein: 14.12

Sweet Potato Fries

Prep Time: 5 Mins   Cook Time: 10 Mins   Serves: 4

Ingredients:

- 2 medium sweet potatoes
- 1 tablespoon olive oil
- 1 tablespoon cornstarch
- 1/2 teaspoon kosher salt
- 1/2 teaspoon ground black pepper
- 1/2 teaspoon garlic powder
- 1/4 teaspoon smoked paprika

Directions:

1. Gather the ingredients.
2. Scrub and peel sweet potatoes.
3. Cut sweet potatoes into evenly sized matchsticks. Make sure they are square on all six sides so they cook evenly, and cut them to a similar in length. Place sticks in refrigerator overnight to dry them out. Or if you're looking to make them faster, just dry off as much of the moisture as possible.
4. Toss sweet potatoes with olive oil, cornstarch, salt, pepper, garlic powder, and paprika in a large bowl until sweet potatoes are completely coated.
5. Heat air fryer to 400°F for 8 minutes. Add sweet potato fries to preheated air fryer basket in one even layer. Do not overlap fries or they will not crisp properly.
6. Cook at 400°F for 8 to 10 minutes. Check after 8 minutes to see if they need to be cooked for longer. (Every air fryer is slightly different). Remove from air fryer and sprinkle with more salt, if needed. Keep warm in a 200°F oven while you prepare the next batch, or eat them right away. Serve hot with your favorite dipping sauces, such as an aioli with garlic or pesto.

Nutritional Value (Amount per Serving):

Calories: 99; Fat: 3.52; Carb: 16.11; Protein: 1.24

Mixed Veggies with Vinaigrette

Prep Time: 10 Mins   Cook Time: 15 Mins   Serves: 4

Ingredients:

- 1 red pepper, cut in 3cm slices
- 1 yellow pepper, cut in 3cm slices
- 2 medium courgettes, cut in 2cm slices
- 1 medium red onion, peeled and petals cut in 5cm pieces
- 5 garlic cloves, peeled and minced
- 2 tbsp olive oil, divided
- Flaked sea salt, to taste
- Fresh cracked black pepper, to taste
- 1 tsp red wine vinegar
- 1 tbsp capers
- 1/4 tsp chilli flakes
- Fresh torn basil

Directions:

1. Insert crisper plate in pan and place pan in unit. Preheat unit by selecting AIR FRY, set temperature to 356°F and set time to 3 minutes. Select START/STOP to begin.
2. In a large bowl, combine red pepper, yellow pepper, courgettes, red onion, garlic, 1 tablespoon olive oil, sea salt and black pepper. Mix well.
3. Once unit has preheated, remove pan and add vegetables to crisping plate. Place pan back in unit and select AIR FRY. Set temperature to 356°F, set time for 15 minutes and select START/ STOP to begin.
4. When cooking is complete, remove pan and place cooked vegetables in a large bowl with vinegar, remaining oil, capers, chilli flakes and basil. Mix well to combine, adjusting seasoning as desired.

Nutritional Value (Amount per Serving):

Calories: 527; Fat: 33.52; Carb: 10.04; Protein: 47.96

Air Fryer Mediterranean Vegetables

Prep Time: 5 Mins   Cook Time: 20 Mins   Serves: 2

Ingredients:

- 1 zucchini sliced into rounds ½ inch thick
- 5 oz cherry tomatoes
- 1 bell pepper diced into medium-large chunks
- ½ red onion diced into medium-large chunks

- 2 Tablespoons olive oil
- 1 teaspoon dried oregano
- ¼ teaspoon smoked paprika
- ½ teaspoon salt
- pepper to taste

Directions:

1. Prep the vegetables (dice the onion and bell pepper, slice the zucchini into thick coins). Add the vegetables to a large bowl.
2. Add the olive oil, oregano, smoked paprika, salt, and a sprinkling of black pepper. Stir until vegetables are coated in the seasoning.
3. Add to the air fryer basket (parchment paper optional). Air fry at 400 degrees F for 15 minutes, tossing every 5 minutes.
4. Serve as desired (I love crumbled feta and fresh parsley or basil).

Nutritional Value (Amount per Serving):

Calories: 206; Fat: 14.53; Carb: 19.79; Protein: 2.22

Air Fryer Zaatar Zucchini

Prep Time: 5 Mins   Cook Time: 15 Mins   Serves: 1

Ingredients:

- 1 zucchini
- 1 tablespoon olive oil
- ½ teaspoon zaatar seasoning

Directions:

1. Cut the ends off the zucchini, then dice into ½ inch cubes.
2. Place the zucchini in a bowl, then toss with the olive oil and zaatar spice.
3. Place in the air fryer, and spread out.
4. Cook for 9-10 minutes at 400 degrees F, shaking halfway through. Check frequently for doneness!
5. Remove and serve.

Nutritional Value (Amount per Serving):

Calories: 126; Fat: 13.54; Carb: 1.15; Protein: 0.36

Air Fryer Asparagus with Lemon

Prep Time: 5 Mins   Cook Time: 13 Mins   Serves: 1

Ingredients:

- 8 oz asparagus
- 1 teaspoon olive oil
- ¼ teaspoon dried oregano
- salt

- pepper
- ½ lemon

Directions:

1. Carefully rinse and dry the asparagus spears. Trim the woody ends off the asparagus.
2. Add asparagus to a large plate. Drizzle the olive oil on top, add the dried oregano, and season with salt and pepper. Gently toss to coat.
3. Place asparagus spears in a single layer in the air fryer basket. Cook at 370°F for 7-9 minutes.
4. Remove from the air fryer, plate, then squeeze fresh lemon juice on top. Season with more salt and pepper to taste.

Nutritional Value (Amount per Serving):

Calories: 109; Fat: 4.93; Carb: 14.92; Protein: 6

Air Fryer Broccolini

Prep Time: 5 Mins   Cook Time: 12 Mins   Serves: 2

Ingredients:

- 8 oz broccolini
- 1 Tablespoon olive oil
- 2 Tablespoons feta
- 1 lemon zest and juice
- salt
- black pepper

Directions:

1. Wash and dry broccolini. Trim bottom ½ inch of stem.
2. Drizzle with olive oil and season with salt and pepper. Toss.
3. Add to air fryer basket in a single layer. Air fry at 380 degrees for 6-9 minutes, checking at the 5 minute mark for doneness.
4. Remove from the air fryer and plate. Top with crumbled feta and fresh lemon zest. Serve with lemon halves for squeezing.

Nutritional Value (Amount per Serving):

Calories: 464; Fat: 38.77; Carb: 8.53; Protein: 21.52

Crispy Air Fryer Brussels Sprouts

Prep Time: 10 Mins   Cook Time: 25 Mins   Serves: 4

Ingredients:

- 1 pound Brussels Sprouts
- 1 tablespoon Olive Oil
- 1/2 teaspoon Salt, adjust to taste
- 1/4 teaspoon Black Pepper, adjust to taste

- 1/2 teaspoon Garlic powder, optional
- 1 tablespoon Balsamic Vinegar, optional

Directions:

1. Rinse brussels sprouts with water to clean and pat dry with a paper towel.
2. Cut the bottom stem, then cut each brussels sprout in half. Place them in a bowl.
3. Toss the brussels sprouts with olive oil, salt, pepper, garlic powder and balsamic vinegar. Transfer them to air fryer basket.
4. Air fry them at 360°F for 10-12 minutes or until they are slightly browned. Shake them half way through.
5. Brussels sprouts are ready. Remove in a serving plate and drizzle with some lime juice. Enjoy as is or with a dip of garlic thyme mayonnaise.

Nutritional Value (Amount per Serving):

Calories: 84; Fat: 3.72; Carb: 11.23; Protein: 3.94

Air Fryer Corn on the Cob

Prep Time: 5 Mins   Cook Time: 20 Mins   Serves: 3

Ingredients:

- 3 ears Sweet Corn on the Cob
- 1 teaspoon Oil, for spraying, optional
- 1 tablespoon vegan butter/oil, softened
- 1/4 teaspoon Kosher Salt
- 1/8 teaspoon Black pepper
- 1/4 teaspoon Kashmiri Red Chili powder, or paprika, optional
- 1/2 Lime, optional
- 1 teaspoon Cilantro, chopped

Directions:

1. Remove the husk and silk from the corn ears. You can rinse the ears to remove any dirt. Then dry with a paper towel. If you like, remove the stems or cut the ears in half.
2. You can either spray with oil or not (The corn can be crispier if you use oil). Then place the corn in the air fryer basket. Cook at 380°F for 13-15 minutes, turning in between at least once.
3. Transfer the cooked corn onto a large plate. Brush with melted butter. Season with salt and pepper. Enjoy as is or make it spicy as below.
4. Optionally, you can mix salt, pepper and red chili powder in a small bowl. Then sprinkle the mixture on the corn. Or use dip half a lime in the spice mix, and rub the lime over the corn. Garnish with chopped cilantro. This is Indian street style spiced corn.

5. Serve immediately while the corn is warm!
Nutritional Value (Amount per Serving):
Calories: 208; Fat: 9.22; Carb: 32.77; Protein: 4.56

Teriyaki Cauliflower Wings

Prep Time: 20 Mins   Cook Time: 50 Mins   Serves: 8

Ingredients:

- 1 medium cauliflower head, chopped into florets
- ½ teaspoon garlic powder
- 1 cup flour (either all-purpose flour or gluten-free all-purpose flour)
- 1 ¼ cup unsweetened non-dairy milk (we use soy milk)
- 2 cups breadcrumbs (use gluten-free if needed)
- Cooking spray
- ½ cup low-sodium soy sauce (or tamari if gluten-free)
- 1 cup water
- 2 tablespoon brown sugar
- 2 tablespoon rice vinegar
- 1 tablespoon toasted sesame oil
- 3 garlic cloves, minced
- 2 tsp minced ginger
- 2 tablespoon corn starch (or sub with arrowroot starch)
- ⅛ teaspoon Freshly cracked black pepper
- A pinch of chili flakes (optional, for heat)

Directions:

1. Preheat air fryer to 350°F.
2. To a medium mixing bowl, mix flour and garlic powder together. Then slowly pour the milk, stirring constantly.
3. To another bowl, add the breadcrumbs. Start coating the cauliflower florets by dipping each one in the wet mixture first, letting any excess batter drip off. Then roll it in the breadcrumbs. Repeat until all florets are coated.
4. Spray the air fryer basket with oil or cooking spray. Add florets to the basket in a single layer, then spray them with oil. Cook for 12-15 minutes, or until golden and crispy. Make sure to stop and shake the basket halfway through.
5. In the meantime, make the teriyaki sauce. Add all of the ingredients to a saucepan- soy sauce, water, sesame oil, rice vinegar, sugar, garlic, ginger, cornstarch, black pepper, and chili flakes (optional). Heat over medium-high heat, stirring occasionally. When the sauce starts to boil, turn the heat to medium-low and start whisking constantly, simmering the sauce for 2-3 minutes until it thickens. Remove from the heat.

6. Add wings to a bowl and pour ⅔ of the sauce. Mix gently. Use the rest of the sauce to drizzle on spots that didn't get coated well. Top with toasted sesame seeds (optional) and serve right away!

Nutritional Value (Amount per Serving):

Calories: 439; Fat: 36.52; Carb: 24.91; Protein: 4.86

Easy Air Fryer Roasted Cauliflower Steak

Prep Time: 10 Mins   Cook Time: 40 Mins   Serves: 4

Ingredients:

- 2 heads Cauliflower - medium to large
- 1 teaspoon Salt
- ½ teaspoon Black Pepper
- ½ teaspoon Sumac - optional dry herb with a citrus flavor
- ½ teaspoon Paprika
- ½ teaspoon Garlic Powder
- Non- Virgin Olive Oil or Avocado oil

Directions:

1. Place cauliflower in colander and rinse clean. Carefully remove outer leaves and trim bottom of stem. Be careful not to remove to much or steak will fall apart.
2. Using a large knife cut the cauliflower in half lengthwise through center. Cut 1 ½ inch steak from each side. Unless you have a very large head of cauliflower each one will produce 2 steaks with leftover's for rice or to steam.
3. Repeat with other head of cauliflower.
4. Place the steaks in a single layer in the inner basket of the air fryer.
5. Set Air Fryer for 350°F degrees.
6. Air fry them for 10 minutes and then flip and then cook for additional 5 to 8 minutes until tender.
7. Note depending on the size of cauliflower the time may vary slightly. Cook until steak are tender.
8. Serve with hummus or quinoa and a side of green beans.

Nutritional Value (Amount per Serving):

Calories: 51; Fat: 2.01; Carb: 7.4; Protein: 2.79

Mediterranean Eggplant Parmesan

Prep Time: 30 Mins   Cook Time: 50 Mins   Serves: 4

Ingredients:

- 2 large eggplants, sliced into 1/2-inch rounds
- 1 cup marinara sauce
- 1 cup vegan mozzarella cheese, shredded
- 1/2 cup vegan Parmesan cheese, grated
- 1/4 cup fresh basil leaves
- 2 tablespoons olive oil
- 1 teaspoon dried oregano
- 1/2 teaspoon garlic powder
- Salt and pepper to taste

Directions:

1. Preheat your air fryer to 380°F.
2. Slice the eggplant into thin slices. Brush both sides of the eggplant slices with olive oil and sprinkle with salt, pepper, dried oregano, and garlic powder.
3. Place the seasoned eggplant slices in the air fryer basket in a single layer. You may need to cook them in batches. Air fry at 380°F for about 10 minutes, flipping the slices halfway through, or until they are tender and slightly crispy.
4. In an oven-safe dish, layer marinara sauce, air-fried eggplant slices, vegan mozzarella cheese, vegan Parmesan cheese, and fresh basil leaves. Repeat the layers as desired.
5. Place the assembled dish in the air fryer. Air fry at 380°F for about 10 minutes or until the cheese is melted and bubbly, and the dish is heated through.
6. Once the Eggplant Parmesan is done, remove it from the air fryer and let it cool for a few minutes. Serve while warm with a side of bread!

Nutritional Value (Amount per Serving):

Calories: 257; Fat: 15.04; Carb: 24.47; Protein: 9.53

Vegan Crunchwrap

Prep Time: 5 Mins   Cook Time: 13 Mins   Serves: 1

Ingredients:

- 1 regular size gluten free tortilla
- 2 tablespoons re-fried pinto beans (or Spicy Vegan Meat Crumbles)
- 2 tablespoons grated vegan cheese or queso sauce
- 1 small corn tortilla
- 2-3 iceberg lettuce leaves
- 2 tablespoons guacamole or sliced avocado
- 2-3 tablespoons salsa

Directions:

1. Preheat air fryer to 325 °F.
2. Assemble each crunch wrap by stacking in this order:
   - large regular tortilla
   - beans or meat
   - grated cheese or cheese sauce
   - small corn tortilla
   - Salsa
   - whole iceberg lettuce leaves
   - guacamole or avocado slices
3. Fold everything together
4. more cheese to 'seal' closed
5. In the air fryer: Cook the Taco Crunch Wrap for 6 minutes at 350°F.

Nutritional Value (Amount per Serving):

Calories: 1632; Fat: 70.9; Carb: 198.29; Protein: 65.9

Air Fryer Falafel

Prep Time: 5 Mins   Cook Time: 20 Mins   Serves: 15

Ingredients:

- 2 cans (14-ounce) organic no salt added chickpeas , rinsed, drained well & patted dry
- 1 small red onion , roughly chopped
- 3 garlic cloves
- 2 tbsp fresh lemon juice
- 1/3 cup fresh parsley
- 1/3 cup fresh cilantro
- 3 tbsp nutritional yeast
- 1 tsp smoked paprika
- 2 tsp ground cumin
- 1 tsp ground coriander
- 3/4 tsp salt
- black pepper
- 2 tbsp superfine blanched almond flour, you can also sub with gluten-free oat flour, chickpea flour or even regular all purpose flour if not gluten-free.
- 1 tsp baking soda

Directions:

1. Place drained chickpeas in a food processor with onion and garlic. Pulse for about 30 seconds until the chickpeas are mostly smooth.
2. Add lemon juice, parsley, coriander, nutritional yeast, paprika, cumin,

ground coriander, salt and pepper. Blend again until smooth and combined. Then stir in the flour and baking soda.

3. Take a tablespoon-sized scoop of the mixture and roll into a ball or form into patties. Repeat with remaining mixture. It should make around 15 falafel. Place the patties in the fridge for 30 minutes (or the freezer for 10 minutes) to firm up.

4. When ready to cook, lightly coat each falafel with avocado oil spray. Working in batches, place patties in a single layer in the air fryer basket. Turn the air fryer to 375°F and cook or 12-13 minutes, flipping each one over half-way through.

5. Best served hot but will keep for 2-3 days in an airtight container in the fridge or freezer for up to 3 months.

Nutritional Value (Amount per Serving):

Calories: 27; Fat: 0.33; Carb: 5.07; Protein: 1.69

Stuffed Portobello Mushrooms

Prep Time: 20 Mins   Cook Time: 35 Mins   Serves: 4

Ingredients:

- 4 large Portobello mushrooms, stems removed
- 1 can (15 oz) chickpeas, drained and rinsed
- 1 cup cooked quinoa or couscous
- 1/2 cup diced tomatoes
- 1/4 cup diced red onion
- 1/4 cup diced cucumber
- 1/4 cup chopped fresh parsley
- 2 tablespoons olive oil
- 2 tablespoons lemon juice
- 1 teaspoon dried oregano
- Salt and pepper to taste
- Olive oil cooking spray

Directions:

1. Preheat your air fryer to 375°F.
2. Clean the Portobello mushrooms and remove the stems. Lightly scoop out the gills to create a cavity for the stuffing.
3. In a bowl, combine the drained chickpeas, cooked quinoa or couscous, diced tomatoes, diced red onion, diced cucumber, chopped fresh parsley, olive oil, lemon juice, dried oregano, salt, and pepper. Mix until well combined.
4. Fill each Portobello mushroom with the prepared stuffing mixture.

5. Lightly grease the air fryer basket with olive oil cooking spray.
6. Place the stuffed Portobello mushrooms in the air fryer basket. Air fry at 375°F for about 12-15 minutes, or until the mushrooms are tender and the stuffing is heated through.
7. Once the stuffed Portobello mushrooms are done, remove them from the air fryer and serve hot. You can garnish them with additional fresh parsley for a pop of color.

Nutritional Value (Amount per Serving):

Calories: 242; Fat: 9.28; Carb: 32.58; Protein: 10.2

Air Fryer Vegan Rolled Tacos

Prep Time: 20 Mins   Cook Time: 30 Mins   Serves: 8

Ingredients:

- 1 large avocado or 2 small ones
- salt & pepper to taste
- 1 15-ounce can vegan refried beans
- 1/2 -1 tbsp taco seasoning
- 8 corn tortillas
- olive oil
- hot sauce
- shredded lettuce, cilantro, salsa, vegan cilantro ranch (optional toppings)

Directions:

1. Scoop the avocado into a bowl and sprinkle with salt & pepper. Mash with a fork and set aside.
2. Add the refried beans and taco seasoning to a bowl and stir to combine. Taste and adjust taco seasoning if needed.
3. Heat your tortillas over an open flame (or in the microwave) and place them in a clean dish towel to keep them warm.
4. Working one at a time, brush one side of the tortilla with olive oil and then flip it over. Add a small amount of avocado to the center, followed by a big scoop of beans and a drizzle of hot sauce. Starting at one end, roll the tortilla up and place it seam side down on a plate or cutting board (the side you brushed with olive oil should be facing out). Repeat with the remaining ingredients.
5. Place the rolled tacos in the air fryer, seam side down. Cook at 380 degrees F for 10 minutes, flipping halfway. Depending on the size of your air fryer you may need to make these in batches. Place the finished rolled tacos on a plate covered with a clean kitchen towel to keep them warm while the second batch cooks.

6. Serve rolled tacos with your favorite taco toppings.

Nutritional Value (Amount per Serving):

Calories: 156; Fat: 6.32; Carb: 21.33; Protein: 4.99

Vegan Stuffed Bell Peppers

Prep Time: 20 Mins   Cook Time: 40 Mins   Serves: 4

Ingredients:

- 4 large bell peppers (any color)
- 1 cup cooked quinoa
- 1 cup canned chickpeas, drained and rinsed
- 1/2 cup diced tomatoes
- 1/2 cup diced cucumber
- 1/4 cup diced red onion
- 1/4 cup diced Kalamata olives
- 1/4 cup chopped fresh parsley
- 2 tablespoons olive oil
- 2 tablespoons lemon juice
- 1 teaspoon ground cumin
- Salt and pepper to taste

Directions:

1. Preheat your air fryer to 375°F.
2. Combine cooked quinoa, chickpeas, diced tomatoes, diced cucumber, diced red onion, Kalamata olives, chopped fresh parsley, olive oil, lemon juice, ground cumin, salt, and pepper. Mix until all ingredients are well combined.
3. Carefully stuff each bell pepper with the Mediterranean filling mixture. Fill them to the top.
4. Place the stuffed bell peppers in the air fryer basket, standing upright. Air fry at 375°F for 15-20 minutes
5. Once the stuffed peppers are done, remove them from the air fryer, let them cool slightly, and serve immediately. Enjoy!

Nutritional Value (Amount per Serving):

Calories: 228; Fat: 9.94; Carb: 29.65; Protein: 7.48

Chapter 3: Poultry

Crispy Mediterranean Air Fryer Chicken Thighs

Prep Time: 15 Mins   Cook Time: 20 Mins   Serves: 6

Ingredients:

- 1.5 to 2 lbs boneless skinless chicken thighs 6 to 8 chicken thighs
- 2 Tbsp olive oil
- Zest and juice of 1 lemon
- 1 tsp Sumac
- 1 tsp ground cumin
- 1 tsp paprika
- 1/2 tsp ground cinnamon
- 1/2 tsp allspice
- 1 tsp kosher salt

Directions:

1. Combine all of the spices in a small bowl (sumac, ground cumin, paprika, ground cinnamon, allspice and sea salt) and stir until incorporated.
2. Pat the chicken dry with a paper towel and place chicken thighs (or breasts) in a large zip lock bag (or freezer bag) and add the olive oil, lemon zest, lemon juice, and the spice blend. Seal the bag and shake everything around until all of the thighs are well-coated in the marinade.
3. Either refrigerate for 15 minutes (up to 24 hours) to marinate, or cook the chicken immediately. For the best results, marinate the chicken for at least 15 minutes. If you don't have time to marinate the chicken, you can toss all of the ingredients in a mixing bowl and toss it all together using your hands.
4. Lightly spray the air fryer basket with cooking spray. Preheat the air fryer to 375 degrees for a few minutes.
5. Place the chicken thighs in the air fryer with the rounded side down in a single layer (do this in two batches if your air fryer is too small to fit the thighs in one layer). Air fry for 14 minutes.
6. Flip the chicken and air fry for an additional 4 to 6 minutes, until the thighs are crispy and cooked through.
7. For chicken breasts, air fry at 350°F for 9 minutes per side. For bone-in chicken thighs, air fry at 375°F for 10 minutes per side.
8. Chicken is considered fully cooked once it reaches an internal temperature of 165 degrees F. To verify the temperature, insert an instant read thermometer into the thickest part of the thigh and wait until the numbers stop moving to get an accurate read. A meat thermometer is the best way of ensuring the chicken thighs turn out perfectly cooked for a delicious meal.
9. Serve Crispy Mediterranean Chicken with your choice of side dishes and enjoy!

Nutritional Value (Amount per Serving):

Calories: 296; Fat: 23.5; Carb: 1.49; Protein: 18.9

Air Fryer Chicken Breast

Prep Time: 2 Mins   Cook Time: 15 Mins   Serves: 2

Ingredients:

- 2 pieces Boneless, Skinless Chicken Breasts, mine were 340 grams
- 55 grams Baba Ganoush, mine was store bought
- 1/4 teaspoon Sea Salt, 1/8 tsp per chicken breast
- 1/4 teaspoon Black Pepper, 1/8 tsp per chicken breast

Directions:

1. Pat the chicken breasts dry with paper towel and place in a small bowl
2. Season chicken breasts with salt and pepper
3. Coat the chicken breasts with baba ganoush
4. Place the chicken breasts on the air fryer basket without overlapping
5. Cook chicken breasts for 15 minutes on 375 degrees Fahrenheit
6. (Optional) When done, remove the air fryer basket and let the chicken breasts rest for 5 minutes.

Nutritional Value (Amount per Serving):

Calories: 47; Fat: 2.02; Carb: 4.38; Protein: 3.08

Air Fryer Greek Chicken Bowls

Prep Time: 10 Mins   Cook Time: 46 Mins   Serves: 4

Ingredients:

Chicken And Marinade
- 2 8-ounce boneless skinless chicken breasts
- 2 tablespoons olive oil
- 2 teaspoons dried oregano
- 1 teaspoon Italian seasoning
- 1 teaspoon kosher salt
- ½ teaspoon ground black pepper
- Juice of half a lemon

Bowls
- 2 cups cooked cauliflower rice
- 1 pint cherry tomatoes rinsed and halved
- 1 cup sliced cucumbers English cucumbers recommended
- ½ cup sliced red onion
- ½ cup reduced fat feta crumbles
- 1 tablespoon fresh chopped dill
- 4 Lemon wedges

- 1 batch skinny tzatziki sauce

Directions:

Marinating The Chicken:

1. In a gallon Ziploc bag or large bowl combine the olive oil, oregano, Italian seasoning, salt, pepper and lemon juice. Add the chicken breasts. Toss to coat and place the chicken into the refrigerator to marinate for at least 30 minutes, or overnight.
2. While the chicken marinates, prepare the tzatziki sauce if not already made. Chill until serving.
3. When ready to cook, remove the chicken from the ziploc bag or bowl and discard the marinade. Lightly spray the air fryer basket with olive oil spray.
4. Place the chicken into the greased air fryer basket and cook on at 370 degrees F for 13-16 minutes (turning it over halfway through) or until the thickest part of the chicken reads an internal temperature of 165F with a food thermometer.
5. Remove the chicken from the air fryer and allow to rest for 2-3 minutes before serving.

Making The Greek Bowls:

1. Divide the cauliflower rice, regular rice rice or grain of your choice between four serving bowls.
2. Divide the following next between the four bowls: halved tomatoes, sliced cucumbers, and red onions.
3. Add one quarter of the sliced chicken on top of each bowl. Spoon the tzatziki sauce across the chicken, and sprinkle on 2 tablespoons of feta crumbles.
4. Garnish with fresh dill and serve with a lemon wedge.

Nutritional Value (Amount per Serving):

Calories: 973; Fat: 42.46; Carb: 69.19; Protein: 96.91

Mediterranean Chicken Leg Quarters

Prep Time: 10 Mins   Cook Time: 30 Mins   Serves: 4

Ingredients:

- 4 pieces chicken leg quarters 2 lbs approx
- 1 tsp salt
- 1 tsp black pepper
- 1 tsp oregano
- 1/2 tsp rosemary
- 1 tsp smoked paprika
- 1/4 tsp cayenne pepper
- 1/4 cup olive oil
- 1 tbsp garlic minced or paste

Directions:

1. Make the marinade by combining all the ingredients listed above (except

chicken leg quarters). Set the marinade aside.

2. Poke holes in the chicken leg quarters.
3. Coat the chicken with the marinade. Be sure to apply it under the skin.
4. Allow the chicken to marinate for 4-6 hours or overnight.
5. Pre-heat your air fryer. Then place the chicken in the air fryer. Cook for 25 to 30 mins at 365°F.
6. Flip the chicken at the halfway mark approx 12-15 min mark and resume cooking.
7. Serve with pita bread, salad or Mediterranean rice.

Nutritional Value (Amount per Serving):

Calories: 862; Fat: 43.9; Carb: 1.74; Protein: 110.92

Air Fryer Chicken Shawarma

Prep Time: 10 Mins   Cook Time: 30 Mins   Serves: 8

Ingredients:

- 3 cloves garlic, minced
- 1 tablespoon coriander
- 1 tablespoon cardamom
- 1/4 teaspoon cayenne pepper
- 1 tablespoon paprika
- 1 teaspoon sumac
- 2 teaspoons sea salt
- 1 whole lemon, juiced
- 1/3 cup avocado oil
- 2 teaspoons sugar
- 2 pounds chicken breast or thighs
- To Make Wraps
- pita bread or flatbread
- tzatziki sauce
- tomato
- green or romaine lettuce
- red onion

Directions:

1. Combine chicken with lemon juice, avocado oil, garlic, coriander, cardamom, cayenne pepper, paprika, sumac, salt, and sugar in a large bowl or gallon ziplock bag.
2. 3 cloves garlic, minced,1 tablespoon coriander,1 tablespoon cardamom,1/4 teaspoon cayenne pepper,1 tablespoon paprika,1 teaspoon sumac,2 teaspoons sea salt,1 whole lemon, juiced,1/3 cup avocado oil,2 teaspoons sugar,2 pounds chicken breast or thighs
3. If in a bag, massage chicken into marinade. If in a bowl, toss to coat well.
4. Leave it in the refrigerator to marinate for at least 24 hours, or store in the freezer for future use.
5. Preheat the air fryer to 375°F.
6. Add chicken (defrosted if you previously froze it) to the air fryer and cook for 7-20 minutes, flipping with five minutes left. How long to cook your shawarma will depend on the thickness of your chicken breasts. Smaller

(7-8 ounces) will take 7-10 minutes, and larger (10-11 ounces) chicken breasts will take 16-20 minutes. Use a thermometer to ensure the chicken reaches a minimum temperature of 165°F.

Nutritional Value (Amount per Serving):

Calories: 344; Fat: 15.95; Carb: 24.2; Protein: 27.27

Healthy Air Fryer Chicken and Veggies

Prep Time: 5 Mins   Cook Time: 20 Mins   Serves: 4

Ingredients:

- 2-3 medium chicken breasts, chopped into bite sized pieces
- 1 cup broccoli florets (fresh or frozen)
- 1 zucchini, chopped
- 1 cup bell pepper, chopped (any colours you like)
- 1/2 onion, chopped
- 2 cloved garlic, minced or crushed
- 2 tablespoons olive oil
- 1/2 teaspoon EACH garlic powder, chili powder, salt, pepper
- 1 tablespoon Italian seasoning, (or spice blend of choice)

Directions:

1. Preheat air fryer to 400°F.
2. Chop the veggies and chicken into small bite-size pieces and transfer to a large mixing bowl.
3. Add the oil and seasoning to the bowl and toss to combine.
4. Add the chicken and veggies to the preheated air fryer and cook for 10 minutes, shaking halfway, or until the chicken and veggies are charred and chicken is cooked through. If your air fryer is small, you may have to cook them in 2-3 batches.

Nutritional Value (Amount per Serving):

Calories: 391; Fat: 23.71; Carb: 4.23; Protein: 38.83

Mexican-Style Air Fryer Stuffed Chicken Breasts

Prep Time: 20 Mins   Cook Time: 30 Mins   Serves: 2

Ingredients:

- 4 extra-long toothpicks
- 4 teaspoons chili powder, divided
- 4 teaspoons ground cumin, divided

- 1 skinless, boneless chicken breast
- 2 teaspoons chipotle flakes
- 2 teaspoons Mexican oregano
- salt and ground black pepper, to taste
- ½ red bell pepper, sliced into thin strips
- ½ onion, sliced into thin strips
- 1 fresh jalapeño pepper, sliced into thin strips
- 2 teaspoons corn oil
- ½ lime, juiced

Directions:

1. Place toothpicks in a small bowl and cover with water; let them soak to keep them from burning while cooking.
2. Mix 2 teaspoons chili powder and 2 teaspoons cumin in a shallow dish.
3. Preheat an air fryer to 400 degrees F.
4. Place chicken breast on a flat work surface. Slice horizontally through the middle. Pound each half using a kitchen mallet or rolling pin until about 1/4-inch thick.
5. Sprinkle each breast half equally with remaining chili powder, remaining cumin, chipotle flakes, oregano, salt, and pepper. Place 1/2 the bell pepper, onion, and jalapeño in the center of 1 breast half. Roll chicken from the tapered end upward and use 2 toothpicks to secure. Repeat with other breast, spices, and vegetables and secure with remaining toothpicks. Roll each roll-up in chili-cumin mixture in the shallow dish while drizzling with olive oil until evenly covered.
6. Place roll-ups in the air fryer basket with the toothpick side facing up. Set timer for 6 minutes.
7. Turn roll-ups over. Continue cooking in the air fryer until juices run clear and an instant-read thermometer inserted into the center reads at least 165 degrees F, about 5 minutes more.
8. Drizzle lime juice evenly on roll-ups before serving.

Nutritional Value (Amount per Serving):

Calories: 1618; Fat: 20.76; Carb: 298.38; Protein: 58.74

Air Fryer Asian-Glazed Boneless Chicken Thighs

Prep Time: 5 Mins   Cook Time: 2 Hrs 35 Mins   Serves: 4

Ingredients:

- 8 boneless, skinless chicken thighs, fat trimmed, 32 oz total
- 1/4 cup low sodium soy sauce
- 2 1/2 tablespoons balsamic vinegar

- 1 tablespoon honey
- 3 cloves garlic, crushed
- 1 teaspoon Sriracha hot sauce
- 1 teaspoon fresh grated ginger
- 1 scallion, green only sliced for garnish

Directions:

1. In a small bowl combine the balsamic, soy sauce, honey, garlic, sriracha and ginger and mix well.
2. Pour half of the marinade (1/4 cup) into a large bowl with the chicken, covering all the meat and marinate at least 2 hours, or as long as overnight.
3. Reserve the remaining sauce for later.
4. Preheat the air fryer to 400°F.
5. Remove the chicken from the marinade and transfer to the air fryer basket.
6. Cook in batches 14 minutes, turning halfway until cooked through in the center.
7. Meanwhile, place the remaining sauce in a small pot and cook over medium-low heat until it reduces slightly and thickens, about 1 to 2 minutes.
8. To serve, drizzle the sauce over the chicken and top with scallions.

Nutritional Value (Amount per Serving):

Calories: 138; Fat: 3.3; Carb: 19.96; Protein: 7.01

Air Fryer Lemon Pepper Chicken Thighs

Prep Time: 5 Mins   Cook Time: 17 Mins   Serves: 3-4

Ingredients:

- 6 boneless, skinless chicken thighs
- 2.5 tablespoon fresh lemon juice (the juice from about 1 whole lemon)
- 1.5 teaspoon black pepper
- 1 teaspoon smoked paprika
- 1 teaspoon garlic powder
- 1/2 teaspoon dried oregano
- 1–2 tablespoon lemon zest (optional for topping)

Directions:

1. Add the chicken thighs and lemon juice to a bowl mix together to coat the chicken. Then add in the spices, stirring to evenly coat the chicken thighs. You can also use your hands to rub it into the chicken. Marinate for 30 minutes.
2. Place the chicken thighs in one layer in the air fryer, you may need to do this in two batches if your air fryer basket isn't large enough to not crowd the thighs.

3. Cook on 400 degrees F. for 12 minutes, flipping halfway through.
4. Remove, garnish with lemon zest and serve with desired vegetables or sides.

Nutritional Value (Amount per Serving):

Calories: 1323; Fat: 43.08; Carb: 160.2; Protein: 70.32

Yogurt Marinated Air Fryer Chicken

Prep Time: 10 Mins   Cook Time: 2 Hrs 25 Mins   Serves: 4

Ingredients:

- chicken breasts, boneless and skinless
- ½ cup greek yogurt, Full fat, low fat, and nonfat will all work as long as it's unflavored and unsweetened. I like to use nonfat greek yogurt.
- 2 tablespoons lemon juice
- 1 tablespoon garlic, minced
- 2 teaspoons dried basil
- ¾ teaspoon salt
- ½ teaspoon onion powder
- ¼ teaspoon black pepper
- ¼ teaspoon crushed red pepper flakes

Directions:

1. Cut chicken breasts horizontally. This will create 8 thin cutlets.
2. In a gallon Ziploc bag or large covered bowl combine chicken and all marinade ingredients. Let marinate for a minimum of 2 hours or as long as 12 hours. (I recommend marinating for 5 to 12 hours. The longer the better to really bring out the lemon flavor.)
3. Preheat air fryer to 375 degrees F.
4. Place chicken cutlets in a single layer in the preheated air fryer so they're not overlapping. Air fry for 10 minutes. Flip chicken. Air fry for another 5 to 10 minutes or until internal temperature reaches 155 to 160 degrees F. Be careful not to overcook. (Temperature AFTER resting should be 165 degrees F.)Final cooking time will vary based on the thickness of your chicken and the model air fryer you're using.

Nutritional Value (Amount per Serving):

Calories: 145; Fat: 6.85; Carb: 2.78; Protein: 17.63

Air Fryer Chicken Milanese with Mediterranean Salad

Prep Time: 15 Mins   Cook Time: 30 Mins   Serves: 4

Ingredients:

- 8 boneless thin sliced chicken breast fillets, about 4 ounces each, 1/4 inch thick
- 1 teaspoon salt
- 1 1/2 cup panko, or gluten-free panko
- 1/3 cup finely grated Parmesan cheese
- 2 large eggs, beaten
- olive oil spray
- 5 cups 1 large head romaine lettuce, chopped
- 1 heirloom tomato, diced
- 1/2 small red onion, chopped
- 2 ounces grated feta cheese, grated from 1 block
- 2 tablespoons fresh lemon juice
- 2 tablespoons red wine vinegar
- 1 tablespoon dried oregano
- 1 garlic clove, grated
- 1/2 teaspoon kosher salt
- 2 tablespoons extra virgin olive oil

Directions:

1. Season the cutlets on both sides with salt.
2. In a shallow bowl combine the bread crumbs and Parmesan cheese.
3. Beat the egg with 1 tablespoon water. Place in a large flat dish. Coat the cutlets with the egg mixture, remove the excess and dip them into crumbs.
4. Place the cutlets on a work surface and spray both sides generously with oil.
5. Air fry in batches 400°F 6 to 7 minutes turning halfway, until the crumbs are golden brown and the center is no longer pink. Divide on 4 plates.
6. Make the dressing: Combine the lemon juice, vinegar, oregano, garlic, and 1/2 teaspoon salt and let sit until the oregano has absorbed some liquid, about 5 minutes. Whisk in the olive oil.
7. While the cutlets are cooking, toss all the lettuce, tomato, red onion and 1/4 teaspoon salt together in a large bowl. Drizzle over the dressing, toss, and divide among the 4 plates of chicken, piling it over the cutlets.
8. Using a box grater, grate 1/2 ounce of the cheese over each salad.

Nutritional Value (Amount per Serving):

Calories: 393; Fat: `4.81; Carb: 46.05; Protein: 26.09

Air Fryer Greek Chicken Recipe

Prep Time: 10 Mins   Cook Time: 55 Mins   Serves: 4

Ingredients:

- 3 chicken breasts - (this is about 18.5oz altogether), chopped into bitesize pieces
- 2 tbsp oil - I use avocado or rapeseed
- 2 cloves garlic - peeled and minced
- ½ tsp dried dill
- 1 tsp dried oregano
- ¼ tsp ground black pepper
- zest and juice of one lemon
- ½ tsp table salt
- 4 warmed Greek flatbread (optional)

Directions:

1. Add the chopped chicken to a bowl or a ziplock bag.
2. Add the oil, garlic, dill, oregano, pepper, lemon zest and juice.
3. Stir together to evenly distribute in the marinade.
4. Allow to marinade for 20-30 minutes (no more than 2 hours or the lemon juice will break down the fibres in the chicken too much – causing it to go a bit mushy).
5. Just before you're ready to cook, sprinkle over the salt and stir together.
6. Place in the air fryer basket and cook at 400°F for 13-15 minutes, until cooked throughout. Give it a shake halfway through cooking.
7. Once cooked, pile into warmed flatbreads along with your favourite toppings. I love to add lettuce, tomatoes, marinated onions, whipped feta and a drizzle of olive oil.

Nutritional Value (Amount per Serving):

Calories: 544; Fat: 27.87; Carb: 8.04; Protein: 62.93

Chapter 4: Beef, Pork and lamb

Air Fryer Kofta Kebab

Prep Time: 5 Mins   Cook Time: 15 Mins   Serves: 3

Ingredients:

- 1 ¼ cups ground beef
- 1 teaspoon Garlic, minced
- ½ teaspoon Greek seasoning
- 1 ¼ cups Red Onion, small diced
- A sprinkle of sumac

Directions:

1. In a large mixing bowl, mix ground beef, garlic, onions, Greek seasoning and sumac.
2. Make 6 oval koftas by rolling the beef mixture.
3. Put raw beef koftas on air fryer basket without overlapping and crowding.
4. Cook koftas in air fryer for 10 minutes at 350°F.

Nutritional Value (Amount per Serving):

Calories: 132; Fat: 5.83; Carb: 7.35; Protein: 12.1

Air Fryer Steak

Prep Time: 2 Mins   Cook Time: 10 Mins   Serves: 2

Ingredients:

- 14 oz Ribeye steak
- 1 tablespoon Olive oil
- 2 tablespoon Italian seasoning
- 4 pinch Sea salt and black pepper

Directions:

1. Drizzle half the oil over the steaks. Season with salt and pepper and sprinkle over half the Italian seasoning. Rub the oil and seasoning into the steak. Flip the steaks over and repeat on the other side.
2. Place the steaks in the air fryer (you may have to do one at a time). Set the temperature to 400°F and cook for 7-9 minutes for medium rare, 10-13 minutes for medium or 14-15 minutes for well-done. Make sure to flip the steak over at the half way point.
3. Transfer the steak to a chopping board and loosely cover with foil. Let the steak rest for 10 minutes before cutting into it.

Nutritional Value (Amount per Serving):

Calories: 494; Fat: 29.55; Carb: 16.95; Protein: 40.8

Air Fryer Pork Chops

Prep Time: 5 Mins   Cook Time: 20 Mins   Serves: 4

Ingredients:

- 4 boneless pork chops, about 1"-thick
- 2 tbsp. extra-virgin olive oil
- 1/2 c. finely grated Parmesan
- 1 tsp. garlic powder
- 1 tsp. kosher salt
- 1 tsp. onion powder
- 1 tsp. smoked paprika
- 1/2 tsp. freshly ground black pepper

Directions:

1. Pat pork chops dry with paper towels, then coat both sides with oil.
2. In a medium bowl, combine Parmesan, garlic powder, salt, onion powder, paprika, and black pepper. Coat both sides of pork chops with Parmesan mixture, pressing to adhere.
3. In an air-fryer basket, arrange pork chops in a single layer. Cook at 375°F, flipping halfway through, until an instant-read thermometer inserted into thickest part of pork chop registers 145°F, about 9 minutes.
4. Let pork chops rest about 10 minutes before serving

Nutritional Value (Amount per Serving):

Calories: 421; Fat: 18.04; Carb: 5.35; Protein: 55.81

Air Fryer Lamb Chops

Prep Time: 5 Mins   Cook Time: 12 Mins   Serves: 4

Ingredients:

- 4 12-oz Lamb Chops
- 1 tbsp Avocado oil
- 1 tsp Dried rosemary
- 1 tsp Dried thyme
- 1 tsp Sea salt
- ¼ tsp Black pepper

Directions:

1. Preheat the air fryer to 400 degrees F.
2. In a large bowl, drizzle the lamb chops with olive oil. Season with rosemary, thyme, salt, and pepper. Turn to coat evenly.
3. Place the lamb chops in the air fryer in a single layer, with the pieces not touching each other, or at most minimally touching. (If your air fryer is too small, cook in two batches.) Cook for 7-8 minutes, turning at 4 minutes.
4. Remove the lamb chops from the air fryer and place on a plate. Let them rest for 5 minutes before serving.

Nutritional Value (Amount per Serving):

Calories: 515; Fat: 26.93; Carb: 0.2; Protein: 68.01

Air Fryer Lamb Meatballs

Prep Time: 5 Mins   Cook Time: 17 Mins   Serves: 4

Ingredients:

- 1 lb ground lamb
- 1 teaspoon ground cumin
- 2 teaspoon granulated onion
- 2 Tablespoon fresh parsley
- ¼ teaspoon ground cinnamon
- Salt and pepper

Directions:

1. In a large bowl, combine the lamb, cumin, onion, parsley, and cinnamon. Mix thoroughly until all the ingredients are evenly incorporated.
2. Form mixture into approximate 1 inch balls.
3. Place lamb meatballs in the air fryer basket and cook at 350°F for 12-15 minutes. Shake the meatballs halfway through.

Nutritional Value (Amount per Serving):

Calories: 280; Fat: 14.38; Carb: 14.1; Protein: 24.7

Air Fryer Steak Bites

Prep Time: 10 Mins   Cook Time: 20 Mins   Serves: 4

Ingredients:

- 4 pre-cut sirloin steak
- 1 tsp Worcestershire sauce or coconut aminos
- 1/2 tsp salt to taste
- 1 tsp ground black pepper to taste
- Oil spray
- 2 tbsp butter or ghee or olive oil
- 3 cloves garlic minced
- 1/2 tsp red pepper flakes
- Squeeze of fresh lemon juice
- Chopped fresh parsley optional garnish

Directions:

1. Preheat the air fryer to 400°F and set the timer to 20 minutes. I like to have a little extra time on the timer whenever use the air fryer, just in case I need more time.
2. While the air fryer is heating, dice the steak and add it to a large bowl, season it with salt and black pepper, and toss it in the Worcestershire sauce. Mix well.
3. When the air fryer is ready, spray or sprinkle with oil and add the steak cubes to the air fryer basket in a single layer and cook them for 10-12

minutes, until browned on the outside.

4. When the steak bites have finished air frying, remove the air fryer basket and tip the steak onto a plate or bowl to rest for 5 minutes. Avoid tipping the air fryer basket while it's attached to the tray as the juices that have gathered in the bottom tray will also pour out.
5. While the steak is resting, melt butter in a pan over medium heat, add the fresh garlic, and sauté for 2-3 minutes.
6. Sprinkle in the crushed red pepper flakes after one minute and continue cooking.
7. To serve, toss the steak bites in the hot garlic butter (you can also dip steak pieces in the garlic butter sauce if you prefer).
8. Garnish with a squeeze of fresh lemon juice and sprinkle with fresh parsley.

Nutritional Value (Amount per Serving):

Calories: 1298; Fat: 83.78; Carb: 4.21; Protein: 124.44

Air Fryer Beef Meatballs

Prep Time: 30 Mins   Cook Time: 45 Mins   Serves: 4

Ingredients:

- 1lb beef mince
- 1 garlic clove, peeled and crushed
- 1 egg, whisked
- 2oz fresh breadcrumbs
- 2 tbsp finely chopped fresh parsley
- 1/2 tsp salt
- 1/4 tsp freshly ground black pepper
- 1 tsp vegetable oil [optional]

Directions:

1. Place all the ingredients, except the oil, in a large mixing bowl and incorporate everything well.
2. Form 2in in diameter meatballs, which will leave you with approximately 12 meatballs, i.e. 3 meatballs per serving.
3. [Optional] Lightly brush each meatball with a bit of oil. (You don't have to. It just means that the meatballs will be slightly dried out on the outside.)
4. Place the meatballs in the air fryer.
5. Cook the meatballs at 355°F for 8 minutes.

Nutritional Value (Amount per Serving):

Calories: 291; Fat: 14.57; Carb: 7.63; Protein: 31.9

Air Fryer Brisket

Prep Time: 10 Mins   Cook Time: 2 Hrs 30 Mins   Serves: 8

Ingredients:

- 4 lb beef brisket
- 3/4 c beef broth
- 1 tbsp chili powder
- 1 tsp salt
- 1/2 tbsp garlic powder
- 1/2 tbsp onion powder
- 1/2 tbsp brown sugar
- 1 bay leaf crushed

Directions:

1. Mix together spices and brown sugar and rub on brisket. Place brisket in preheated air fryer, fat cap side up, and cook at 350°F for 30 minutes.
2. Lift out meat at this time. Place brisket in foil, fat cap side up. The best way to wrap the brisket is to place two pieces of foil that cross over each other. Pour in broth. Fold up the sides so that the beef stock / broth will not leak out.
3. Place again in air fryer and cook at 300°F for 2 hours or until thickest part of brisket temp registers 195°F. (timing will vary depending on size and thickness of meat)
4. Remove, allow to rest for 10 minutes before slicing against the grain and serving with broth over the top.

Nutritional Value (Amount per Serving):

Calories: 465; Fat: 33.79; Carb: 3.79; Protein: 33.72

Air Fryer Steak Fajitas

Prep Time: 15 Mins   Cook Time: 38 Mins   Serves: 6

Ingredients:

- 1½ pounds sirloin tip steak sliced into thin strips
- ¼ teaspoon chili powder
- ½ teaspoon onion powder
- ½ teaspoon garlic powder
- ½ teaspoon ground cumin
- ½ teaspoon salt
- ¼ teaspoon ground black pepper
- ½ cup Worcestershire sauce
- 2 cloves of garlic minced
- 2 red bell peppers thinly sliced lengthwise
- 1 yellow bell peppers thinly sliced lengthwise
- 1 orange bell peppers thinly sliced lengthwise
- ½ yellow or white onion diced or sliced
- 2 tablespoons olive oil
- ½ teaspoon smoked paprika
- ½ teaspoon salt
- ¼ teaspoon ground black pepper

- Soft tortillas shells
- Lime
- Avocado slices

Directions:

1. In a medium mixing bowl, combine the steak strips with the seasonings.
2. Add Worcestershire sauce, and minced garlic. And allow to marinate for at least 15 minutes, but preferably for longer (2 hours or even overnight).
3. Toss the bell peppers and onions with olive oil, smoked paprika, salt and pepper.
4. Preheat the Air Fryer to 400°F for 5 minutes, when it's hot, remove the steak strips using a pair of tongs (discard the marinade), and add the steak to the air fryer basket along with the fajita veggies.
5. Air fry for 8 minutes shaking the basket halfway through.
6. After cooking, assemble the fajitas inside soft tortilla shells. Top with avocado slices, a squeeze of fresh lime juice or any other fajita toppings of your choosing.

Nutritional Value (Amount per Serving):

Calories: 386; Fat: 22; Carb: 13.3; Protein: 33.72

Chapter 5: Fish and Seafood

Air Fryer Pesto Salmon

Prep Time: 3 Mins   Cook Time: 13 Mins   Serves: 1

Ingredients:

- 6 oz salmon fillet
- ½ teaspoon olive oil plus extra for brushing/spraying on air fryer basket
- salt
- pepper
- 2 teaspoons pesto

Directions:

1. Pat your salmon fillet dry with paper towels. Drizzle olive oil over the surface of the salmon and rub in. Sprinkle with salt and pepper.
2. Add pesto to the top of the salmon. Spread over the top.
3. Brush or spray the air fryer basket with extra oil to prevent salmon from sticking.
4. Add salmon to the air fryer basket and cook for 8-12 minutes at 400 degrees F, until salmon is cooked through and flaky.
5. Remove from air fryer and enjoy!

Nutritional Value (Amount per Serving):

Calories: 470; Fat: 32.18; Carb: 5.54; Protein: 39.12

Air Fryer Pesto Shrimp

Prep Time: 3 Mins   Cook Time: 9 Mins   Serves: 2

Ingredients:

- 12 raw shrimp medium-sized, deveined
- 2 Tablespoons pesto

Directions:

1. Dry the shrimp on paper towels.
2. Add the shrimp and pesto to a large bowl. Toss gently until shrimp is coated in the pesto.
3. Add shrimp in a single layer to the air fryer. Cook at 400 degrees F for 6-8 minutes.

Nutritional Value (Amount per Serving):

Calories: 111; Fat: 9.16; Carb: 0.97; Protein: 6.46

Air Fryer Harissa Salmon

Prep Time: 5 Mins   Cook Time: 15 Mins   Serves: 1

Ingredients:

- 6 oz salmon
- 1 Tablespoon harissa
- ½ lemon
- 1 teaspoon honey
- salt
- pepper

Directions:

1. Dry the salmon with paper towels. Season with a sprinkling of salt and pepper.
2. In a small bowl, add harissa, honey, and juice from ½ a lemon. Stir to combine.
3. Add the harissa sauce over the salmon. Place the salmon in the air fryer basket.
4. Cook at 380 degrees F for 7-10 minutes. Remove from the air fryer and enjoy.

Nutritional Value (Amount per Serving):

Calories: 305; Fat: 12.34; Carb: 11.76; Protein: 36.1

Air Fryer Mediterranean Salmon

Prep Time: 5 Mins   Cook Time: 15 Mins   Serves: 1

Ingredients:

- 6 oz salmon fillet
- 1 teaspoon olive oil
- ⅛ teaspoon garlic powder
- ½ teaspoon oregano or Italian seasoning
- ¼ lemon
- salt
- pepper

Directions:

1. Pat the salmon fillet dry with paper towels and remove any bones. Place on a plate. Drizzle the fillet with olive oil and rub into the surface.
2. Season the salmon with salt and pepper. Then sprinkle the garlic powder over the top, then the oregano.
3. Either brush or spray the air fryer basket with oil, or use air fryer parchment paper. Place the salmon in the air fryer basket.
4. Cook at 400 degrees for 7-10 minutes. (Cook time may vary based on the thickness of salmon).
5. Plate, then squeeze fresh lemon juice over the salmon.

Nutritional Value (Amount per Serving):

Calories: 323; Fat: 16.84; Carb: 5.72; Protein: 36.14

Air Fryer Whole Fish

Prep Time: 30 Mins   Cook Time: 60 Mins   Serves: 2

Ingredients:

- 1-2 large bream gutted and de-scaled
- 2 tablespoon seafood seasoning
- ½ teaspoon jerk seasoning paste
- 1 teaspoon paprika
- 1 tablespoon lime juice
- 2 tablespoon olive oil
- a splash of water
- 2-3 cups mixed vegetables tightly packed

Directions:

1. Place the fish on a chopping board.
2. Use kitchen scissors to trim off the dorsal and pectoral fins and discard.
3. Use a sharp knife to make 3-4 diagonal scores, leaving a 3-4cm gap between each line on each side of the fish. (be careful not to cut too deep into the fishes cavity).
4. In a small bowl mix together the olive oil, lime juice, jerk seasoning paste and seafood seasoning and add a splash of water if the paste is too thick.
5. Before applying the wet rub to the fish, do a taste test as you may want to add additional pink salt and black pepper.
6. Use your hands (with gloves) or a pastry brush to thoroughly coat the fish with the wet rub including the scores and the cavity too.
7. Leave the fish to marinate for 1-2 hours (or overnight in the refrigerator if you wish to).
8. Preheat your air fryer.
9. Once the air fryer is preheated, place some parchment paper or a liner in the basket.
10. Place the fish in the basket.
Air fry the fish for 25-30 minutes at 375°F.
11. Half way through the cooking time turn the fish over, using an egg spatula to lessen the chances of the fish breaking up.
12. Continue to air fry the fish and about 10 minutes before the finishing time add the vegetables of your choice to the basket.
13. Once everything is cooked, sprinkle the vegetables with the seafood seasoning and serve.

Nutritional Value (Amount per Serving):

Calories: 258; Fat: 14.54; Carb: 30.99; Protein: 1.01

Air Fryer Garlic Butter Salmon

Prep Time: 5 Mins   Cook Time: 15 Mins   Serves: 2

Ingredients:

- 2 (6-ounce) boneless, skin-on salmon fillets (preferably wild-caught)
- 1 1/2 tablespoons butter, melted
- 1 teaspoon garlic, minced
- 1 teaspoon fresh Italian parsley, chopped (or 1/4 teaspoon dried)
- salt and pepper to taste

Directions:

1. Preheat the air fryer to 360 degrees F.
2. Season the fresh salmon with salt and pepper then mix together the melted butter, garlic, and parsley in a bowl.
3. Baste the salmon fillets with the garlic butter mixture and carefully place the salmon inside the air fryer side-by-side with the skin side down.
4. Cook for approximately 10 minutes until salmon flakes easily with a knife or fork.
5. Eat immediately or store up to 3 days using the reheating directions below.

Nutritional Value (Amount per Serving):

Calories: 963; Fat: 37.31; Carb: 107.7; Protein: 47.27

Air Fryer Mahi Mahi

Prep Time: 5 Mins   Cook Time: 17 Mins   Serves: 2

Ingredients:

- 1 to 1 1/2 pounds mahi mahi fillets
- 2 tablespoons olive oil
- 2 cups panko breadcrumbs
- 1 teaspoon paprika
- 1/2 teaspoon garlic powder
- 1/2 teaspoon onion powder
- 1/2 teaspoon salt
- 1/2 teaspoon pepper
- Lemon wedges, for serving

Directions:

1. Preheat your air fryer to 400 degrees F.
2. Place the mahi mahi fillets on a large plate and drizzle or baste with olive oil.
3. In a shallow dish, mix the panko breadcrumbs, paprika, garlic powder, onion powder, salt, and pepper.
4. Dip each mahi mahi fillet into the panko mixture then place in a single layer in the air fryer basket. Spritz with cooking oil.
5. Cook for 12 to 15 minutes, flipping the mahi mahi halfway through cooking.

6. Remove them from the air fryer, serve with lemon wedges, and enjoy!

Nutritional Value (Amount per Serving):

Calories: 888; Fat: 55.73; Carb: 42.11; Protein: 55.93

Air Fryer Cod

Prep Time: 10 Mins   Cook Time: 20 Mins   Serves: 4

Ingredients:

- 4 cod loins
- 4 tablespoons butter, melted
- 6 cloves of garlic, minced
- 2 tablespoons lemon juice (1 lemon)
- 1 teaspoon dried dill (or 2 tablespoons fresh dill, chopped)
- 1/2 teaspoon salt

Directions:

1. Preheat your air fryer to 370 degrees F.
2. Mix the butter, garlic, lemon juice, dill, and salt in a bowl.
3. Add a cod loin into the bowl coating it completely. Lightly press the garlic into the cod so it doesn't fall off when cooking. Repeat with remaining cod pieces.
4. Place all the cod loins into the air fryer in one layer not touching.
5. Cook for 10 minutes then carefully remove from the air fryer.
6. Garnish the cod with more lemon juice or butter if desired and enjoy!

Nutritional Value (Amount per Serving):

Calories: 1682; Fat: 60.56; Carb: 2.31; Protein: 264

Air Fryer Shrimp

Prep Time: 5 Mins   Cook Time: 13 Mins   Serves: 4

Ingredients:

- 1 pound medium raw shrimp, peeled and deveined
- 1/2 cup olive oil
- 2 tablespoons lemon juice
- 1 teaspoon black pepper
- 1/2 teaspoon salt

Directions:

1. Preheat your air fryer to 400 degrees F.
2. Place the shrimp in a Ziploc bag with olive oil, lemon juice, salt, and

pepper. Carefully combine all ingredients.

3. Add parchment paper round (if using) and place the raw shrimp inside the air fryer in one layer.
4. Cook for about 8 minutes, shaking the basket halfway through. The shrimp are done when the shrimp turns bright pink but is still just slightly white, but still a little opaque.
5. Remove the shrimp from the air fryer and enjoy!

Nutritional Value (Amount per Serving):

Calories: 323; Fat: 28.19; Carb: 2.02; Protein: 15.54

Air Fryer Tuna Steaks

Prep Time: 20 Mins   Cook Time: 24 Mins   Serves: 2

Ingredients:

- 2 (6 ounce) boneless and skinless yellowfin tuna steaks
- 1/4 cup soy sauce
- 2 teaspoons honey
- 1 teaspoon grated ginger
- 1 teaspoon sesame oil
- 1/2 teaspoon rice vinegar
- green onions, sliced (optional)
- sesame seeds (optional)

Directions:

1. Remove the tuna steaks from the fridge.
2. In a large bowl, combine the soy sauce, honey, grated ginger, sesame oil, and rice vinegar.
3. Place tuna steaks in the marinade and let marinate for 20-30 minutes covered in the fridge.
4. Preheat air fryer to 380 degrees F and then cook the tuna steaks in one layer for 4 minutes.
5. Let the air fryer tuna steaks rest for a minute or two, then slice, and enjoy immediately! Garnish with green onions and/or sesame seeds if desired.

Nutritional Value (Amount per Serving):

Calories: 552; Fat: 31.16; Carb: 16.43; Protein: 49.7

Air Fryer Scallops

Prep Time: 10 Mins   Cook Time: 15 Mins   Serves: 4

Ingredients:

- 1/2 cup Italian breadcrumbs
- 1/2 teaspoon garlic powder
- 1/4 teaspoon salt
- 1/2 teaspoon black pepper
- 2 tablespoons butter, melted
- 1 pound sea scallops, patted dry

Directions:

1. Preheat your air fryer to 390 degrees F.
2. In a shallow bowl, mix the breadcrumbs, garlic powder, salt, and pepper together. Pour melted butter into a second shallow bowl.
3. Dredge each scallop through the melted butter, then roll in the breadcrumb mixture until they're completely coated; set aside on a plate.
4. Lightly spray the preheated air fryer basket with cooking spray. Arrange scallops in a single layer, working in batches if necessary.
5. Air fry the scallops for 2 minutes. Use tongs to carefully flip them over, then air fry for 3 more minutes until opaque and golden brown.

Nutritional Value (Amount per Serving):

Calories: 181; Fat: 6.74; Carb: 7.14; Protein: 23.73

Air Fryer Salmon Bites

Prep Time: 5 Mins   Cook Time: 10 Mins   Serves: 3-4

Ingredients:

- 1 pound skinless salmon filet
- 1 tablespoon olive oil
- 1 teaspoon lemon juice
- 1 teaspoon garlic powder
- 1 teaspoon onion powder
- ½ teaspoon kosher salt
- ½ teaspoon smoked paprika
- ¼ teaspoon black pepper

For Sriracha Dip:
- ¼ cup mayonnaise
- ½-1 tablespoon sriracha (or ketchup)
- 1 teaspoon lemon juice
- ¼ teaspoon garlic powder

Directions:

1. Cut the salmon into even 1-1.5-inch cubes and place them in a large mixing bowl. Preheat the air fryer to 390 degrees F.
2. Drizzle the oil and lemon juice over the salmon and sprinkle with the seasoning. Use your hands or a wooden spoon to toss everything together, coating the bites completely.
3. Then place the seasoned salmon bites in a single layer in the basket. Air fry for 7-10 minutes, flipping once until fully cooked.
4. While the fish is cooking, combine the dip ingredients in a small mixing bowl and whisk until fully combined. Serve fish immediately with dipping sauce.

Nutritional Value (Amount per Serving):

Calories: 262; Fat: 16.34; Carb: 2.97; Protein: 24.61

Air Fryer Crab Cakes

Prep Time: 5 Mins   Cook Time: 15 Mins   Serves: 4

Ingredients:

- 8 ounces lump crab meat
- 1 red bell pepper, de-seeded and chopped
- 3 green onions, chopped
- 3 tablespoons mayonnaise
- 3 tablespoons breadcrumbs
- 2 teaspoons Old Bay Seasoning
- 1 teaspoon lemon juice
- Lemon wedges, for serving

Directions:

1. Preheat your air fryer to 370 degrees F.
2. In a large bowl, add the lump crab meat, pepper, green onions, mayonnaise, breadcrumbs, Old Bay Seasoning, and lemon juice and mix until just combined.
3. Gently form four evenly sized crab patties. Lump crab meat has a lot of juices inside and you want to keep as much in as possible.
4. Place a piece of parchment round down inside the hot air fryer then carefully place each crab cake in the air fryer.
5. Cook the fresh crab cakes in the air fryer for 8-10 minutes until the crust turns golden brown. Do not flip while cooking.
6. Remove the crab cakes from your air fryer and enjoy with your favorite sauce and extra lemon on top, if desired!

Nutritional Value (Amount per Serving):

Calories: 326; Fat: 6.71; Carb: 44.01; Protein: 26.08

Air Fryer Haddock

Prep Time: 10 Mins   Cook Time: 20 Mins   Serves: 4

Ingredients:

- 4 6 oz haddock filets, skinless
- 1 tablespoon olive oil
- 1 teaspoon Italian seasoning
- ½ teaspoon garlic powder
- ½ teaspoon paprika
- ½ teaspoon kosher salt
- ¼ teaspoon black pepper
- Lemon wedges, for serving
- Serve With: greens, rice, pasta, fresh steamed vegetables

Directions:

1. Pat the fish dry with paper towels and place them on a cutting board.
2. Drizzle the fillets with oil, then sprinkle them on the fleshy sides liberally with the seasonings.
3. Place the filets in a single layer in the air fryer without overcrowding.
4. Air fry at 350 degrees F for 8-10 mins, until fully cooked and opaque. Serve as desired.

Nutritional Value (Amount per Serving):

Calories: 277; Fat: 5.4; Carb: 12.12; Protein: 44.44

Air Fryer Shrimp Fajitas

Prep Time: 5 Mins   Cook Time: 14 Mins   Serves: 4

Ingredients:

- 1 pound raw shrimp thawed
- 3 small mixed bell peppers sliced
- 1 small yellow onion sliced
- 1 tablespoon vegetable oil divided
- 1 tablespoon fajita seasoning divided

For Serving:
- 4 tortillas
- pico de gallo
- 1 avocado sliced
- lime crema

Directions:

1. Preheat the air fryer to 375°F for 5 minutes.
2. Meanwhile, season the vegetables. Toss with half of the oil and half of the fajita seasoning. Add the vegetables to the Air Fryer basket and Air fry for 3 minutes.
3. As the vegetables are being air fried, season the shrimp with the rest of the oil and fajita seasoning.
4. When the 3 minutes are up, with a spatula move the vegetables to one side of the air fryer basket, and add the shrimp to the other half.
5. Air fry for 6 minutes at 375°F flipping halfway through. Mix everything together and serve.
6. Assemble the fajitas over tortillas, and top with your favorite toppings (pico de gallo, guacamole or avocado slices, and lime crema).

Nutritional Value (Amount per Serving):

Calories: 415; Fat: 19.49; Carb: 36.17; Protein: 28.91

Air Fryer Catfish

Prep Time: 40 Mins   Cook Time: 60 Mins   Serves: 2

Ingredients:

- 2 catfish fillets
- 1 cup milk (or buttermilk)
- ½ tablespoon olive oil
- 1 ½ tablespoons blackening seasoning (or Cajun seasoning)
- ½ teaspoon dried oregano
- ½ teaspoon kosher salt
- ½ teaspoon black pepper
- ½ teaspoon garlic powder
- ¼ teaspoon cayenne pepper
- Lemon wedges, for serving
- Fresh chopped parsley, for garnish

Directions:

1. At least 30 minutes before cooking, place the catfish fillets in a plastic zipper bag or large bowl and pour the milk (or buttermilk) over it, allowing it to soak to remove the fishy flavor.
2. In a small bowl, combine the blackening or Cajun seasoning, oregano, salt, pepper, garlic powder, and cayenne pepper then set it aside.
3. When ready to cook, preheat your air fryer to 400 degrees F. Remove the fish and pat it dry. Drizzle the fillets with olive oil. Sprinkle the spice mixture onto both sides of each fillet, coating them completely.
4. Place the fillets in a single layer inside. Spray the tops of the fish.
5. Air fry at 400 degrees F for 10 minutes. Carefully flip the fish and fry for another 10 to 12 minutes (20 to 22 minutes total), until it reaches your desired doneness. Serve with lemon wedges and garnished with parsley.

Nutritional Value (Amount per Serving):

Calories: 298; Fat: 12.25; Carb: 14.47; Protein: 31.41

Chapter 6: Snacks and Appetizers

Air Fryer Parmesan Tomatoes

Prep Time: 5 Mins   Cook Time: 15 Mins   Serves: 4

Ingredients:

- 1 tomato large
- 2 teaspoons olive oil
- ½ teaspoon dried oregano
- salt
- pepper
- ¼ cup parmesan cheese freshly grated
- basil leaves optional

Directions:

1. Slice your tomato into thick slices. Spread the slices out on a cutting board.
2. Drizzle the olive oil over the slices. Season with oregano, salt, and pepper.
3. Grate the parmesan cheese, then top the tomato slices with the cheese.
4. Carefully add the tomato slices to the air fryer basket in a single layer.
5. Cook at 380 degrees F for 10 minutes, checking frequently for doneness.
6. Remove from the air fryer and top with fresh basil leaves.

Nutritional Value (Amount per Serving):

Calories: 56; Fat: 4.19; Carb: 3.15; Protein: 2.02

Air Fryer Greek Potatoes

Prep Time: 10 Mins   Cook Time: 25 Mins   Serves: 4

Ingredients:

- 1 pound small baby potatoes
- 2 Tablespoons olive oil
- 1 Tablespoon dried oregano
- 1 teaspoon garlic powder
- ½ teaspoon salt
- ¼ teaspoon black pepper
- ½ lemon juice

Directions:

1. Wash and scrub the potatoes. Dry, then slice each one in half and place in a large bowl.
2. Add the olive oil, oregano, garlic powder, salt, and pepper to the bowl and toss to combine.
3. Preheat the air fryer for 5 minutes at 400 degrees F.
4. Add the potatoes to the air fryer basket and cook for 15-17 minutes, tossing every 5 minutes until potatoes are soft inside when pierced with a fork.
5. Plate, and then squeeze the juice from ½ a lemon over the top of the potatoes. Serve with extra lemon wedges.

Nutritional Value (Amount per Serving):

Calories: 153; Fat: 6.9; Carb: 21.21; Protein: 2.5

Air Fryer Tomatoes and Onions

Prep Time: 5 Mins   Cook Time: 17 Mins   Serves: 2

Ingredients:

- 2 roma tomatoes
- ½ red onion
- 1 Tablespoon olive oil
- ½ teaspoon dried oregano or Italian seasoning
- ¼ teaspoon salt
- red pepper flakes optional

Directions:

1. Slice a red onion in half and remove the skin. Dice the onion into 1 inch pieces, leaving layers together. Dice the tomatoes into 1 inch pieces.
2. Add the diced tomato and onion to a bowl. Add the olive oil, oregano, salt, and red pepper flakes (optional) to the bowl. Stir to combine.
3. Add tomatoes and onions to air fryer basket. Cook for 12 minutes at 400 degrees F, tossing halfway through cooking.
4. Plate, and top with any fresh herbs if desired.

Nutritional Value (Amount per Serving):

Calories: 98; Fat: 7.1; Carb: 8.25; Protein: 2.03

Mediterranean Diet Air Fried Zucchini Chips

Prep Time: 10 Mins   Cook Time: 18 Mins   Serves: 4

Ingredients:

- 2 Zucchinis - rinsed and with ends cut.
- 2 Eggs
- ¾ cup Almond Flour
- ½ cup Parmesan Cheese – grated
- 2 tsp Seasonings of your preference

Directions:

1. Carefully slice the zucchini if you have not done so. If your slices seem very watery then you can place them on a stack of paper towels or clean kitchen towel for about fifteen minutes to dry out a bit.
2. In a shallow bowl, beat or whip your eggs.

3. Next, in a second shallow bowl, use a whisk or a fork to mix together the almond flour, the seasonings and the cheese Preheat your air fryer to 400 and lightly spray the basket.
4. Use a fork to dip the first sliced zucchini piece into the egg bowl and then dip the chip into the flour mixture.
5. Place the chip into the basket of your air fryer. Repeat this process until you can fill the basket without overcrowding the chips.
6. Lightly spray the chips with a bit of oil. Air fry for eight minutes, stopping to flip the chips at four minutes or until crisp.
7. Repeat the process until you are done making all of the chips.

Nutritional Value (Amount per Serving):

Calories: 222; Fat: 10.31; Carb: 20.44; Protein: 11.05

Crispy Air Fryer Tofu Nuggets with Mediterranean Marinade

Prep Time: 5 Mins   Cook Time: 45 Mins   Serves: 2

Ingredients:

- 14 oz extra firm Tofu
- 3 tablespoons corn starch divided in half
- 2 tablespoon olive oil or any other oil (sesame, peanut, avocado)
- 2 tablespoon balsamic vinegar
- 2 teaspoon garlic powder
- 2 teaspoon oregano dried, or basil, thyme
- 1 tablespoon basil dried
- 1 teaspoon Fine sea salt
- ¼ teaspoon hot paprika or ground black pepper (Optional)
- oil spray (optional)

Directions:

1. Press extra firm tofu for at least 15 minutes (best 30 minutes). Then cut the tofu into cubes.
2. In a small bowl, mix balsamic vinegar and salt.
3. Stir the pressed tofu cubes into the bowl, followed by olive oil, garlic powder, oregano, paprika, or ground pepper (if using).
4. Coat everything evenly but delicately with your hands or spatula.
5. Leave marinating for 15 minutes.
6. Add the tofu cubes into a plastic bag. Stir in the cornstarch and gently shake with your hands- so it sticks to the tofu cubes but doesn't become a paste.
7. Cover the air fryer basket with parchment paper and distribute the seasoned tofu cubes evenly in a single layer, leaving room between each of

them.

8. Bake at 400°F for 15 minutes, shaking the air fryer basket- or moving them carefully with kitchen tongs, halfway.
9. Serve in your favorite buddha bowl, stir fry, or eat as an appetizer with your favorite dipping sauce or on top of a green salad.

Nutritional Value (Amount per Serving):

Calories: 451; Fat: 33.19; Carb: 21.76; Protein: 21.93

Air Fryer Cauliflower

Prep Time: 5 Mins   Cook Time: 12 Mins   Serves: 4

Ingredients:

- 1 head Cauliflower (cut into florets)
- 3 tbsp Olive oil
- 2 tsp Lemon juice
- 3/4 tsp Smoked paprika
- 1/2 tsp Garlic powder
- 1/2 tsp Sea salt
- 1/4 tsp Black pepper

Directions:

1. Preheat the air fryer to 380 degrees F.
2. Place the cauliflower florets in a large bowl. Drizzle with olive oil and lemon juice. Season with smoked paprika, garlic powder, sea salt, and black pepper. Toss to coat.
3. Add cauliflower to the air fryer basket in a single layer (cook in batches if needed – don't crowd the basket). Cook cauliflower in the air fryer for 7-10 minutes (depending on the size of your florets), shaking the basket halfway through, until browned on the edges.

Nutritional Value (Amount per Serving):

Calories: 1202; Fat: 107.03; Carb: 49.65; Protein: 17.13

Air Fryer Pita Chips

Prep Time: 5 Mins   Cook Time: 13 Mins   Serves: 4

Ingredients:

- 2 pita breads
- 1 tablespoon olive oil
- salt
- black pepper
- Toppings:
- 2 teaspoon Zaatar
- 2 teaspoon parsley flakes
- 2 teaspoon Italian seasoning

Directions:

1. Place the pita bread on a cutting board and cut it into 8 pieces or more.

Using a pastry brush or cooking spray, oil both sides of the pita. Mix salt and black pepper together in a small bowl and sprinkle on top of the pita.

2. Alternatively, you can add the pita strips, oil, salt and pepper to a bowl or a large bag and toss to coat. Make sure all the pita strips are evenly coated.
3. Sprinkle either Za'atar, dried parsley or Italian seasoning on the pita strips.
4. Place the pita in the Air fryer basket.

Air fry at 320°F for 7 to 8 minutes until golden and crisp.

Nutritional Value (Amount per Serving):

Calories: 75; Fat: 3.57; Carb: 9.03; Protein: 1.42

Air Fryer BBQ flavoured Chickpeas

Prep Time: 5 Mins   Cook Time: 17 Mins   Serves: 3

Ingredients:

- 15.5 oz can Garbanzo beans drained
- Oil for spraying

For seasoning:
- 1 ½ teaspoon paprika

- 1 teaspoon brown sugar
- ½ teaspoon celery salt
- ½ teaspoon garlic powder
- ½ teaspoon dry mustard
- ¼ teaspoon black pepper

Directions:

1. Place chickpeas in Air Fryer basket. Set temperature to 390 degrees Fahrenheit and timer to 17 minutes. After 5 minutes, open basket and spray chickpeas with oil and shake basket. Close and continue air frying, shaking about every 5 minutes.
2. With about 2 minutes left, open air fryer basket and sprinkle half of the seasoning on the chickpeas. Close and continue air frying for the remaining 2 minutes. Once chickpeas are done, remove and place in a bowl. Sprinkle remainder of the seasoning on the chickpeas and stir to combine. Serve and enjoy.

Nutritional Value (Amount per Serving):

Calories: 257; Fat: 8.79; Carb: 35.97; Protein: 10.69

Parmesan Herb Air Fryer Sweet Potatoes

Prep Time: 10 Mins   Cook Time: 27 Mins   Serves: 4

Ingredients:

- 2 medium-large sweet potatoes
- 2 tablespoons avocado oil

- 1 1/2 teaspoons Italian seasoning
- 1 teaspoon garlic powder

- 1/2 teaspoon salt
- 1 cup grated Parmesan

Directions:

1. Wash exterior of sweet potatoes well then slice into rounds about 1/8" thick. Place in a large bowl.
2. Combine the spices and cheese in a small bowl.
3. Drizzle the sweet potatoes with the oil then toss well to fully coat each round.
4. Add the Parmesan herb mixture to the bowl and toss again to distribute the mixture among the sweet potatoes.
5. Arrange the seasoned sweet potatoes in your air fryer in a single layer either on trays for oven models or in the basket. Work in batches if necessary.
6. Air fry at 400°F for 15 minutes until edges are crispy and middles are fork tender. The tops of the sweet potato rounds should be golden brown.
7. Best served immediately.

Nutritional Value (Amount per Serving):

Calories: 199; Fat: 8.11; Carb: 22.57; Protein: 9.21

Air Fryer Plantain Chips

Prep Time: 10 Mins   Cook Time: 25 Mins   Serves: 2

Ingredients:

- 2 Raw Plantain
- 2 tablespoons Vegetable oil/coconut oil
- 1 ½ teaspoon Salt
- 2 teaspoon Turmeric powder (divided)
- ½ teaspoon Chili flakes (optional)
- 1 cup of water for soaking

Directions:

1. Wash and peel the raw plantains. After that carefully slice the plantains with the help of a slicer for uniform shape and size.
2. Take a half bowl of cool water to add salt and turmeric. Stir it until the salt gets completely dissolved.
3. Place the peeled plantains into the salt and turmeric water for 10 minutes.
4. Remove the plantains from the salt and turmeric water. Pat dry the plantains with a clean kitchen towel or paper towel.
5. Now take a mixing bow to add oil and ½ teaspoon turmeric. Mix it well.
6. Add the plantains slices into the mixture and coat them well.
Preheat your air fryer at 350°F for 5 minutes.
7. Place the coated plantains in the air fryer basket in a single layer.
Cook the air fryer plantain chips at 350°F for 15-20 minutes. Toss the

plantain chips halfway through the cooking process for the evenly cooked result.

8. Remove the air-fried plantain chips, and season with some salt and chili flakes according to your liking.
9. Serve and enjoy.

Nutritional Value (Amount per Serving):

Calories: 310; Fat: 14.07; Carb: 50.33; Protein: 1.6

Crispy Air Fryer Zucchini Chips

Prep Time: 10 Mins   Cook Time: 25 Mins   Serves: 2

Ingredients:

- 1 large zucchini, very thinly sliced (use a mandoline)
- ½ Tablespoon olive oil

Directions:

Preheat air fryer at 270°F for 2 minutes
1. Place the zucchini slices in one single layer between paper towels to help draw out the liquid.
2. Place the zucchini slices in a single layer in the air fryer basket.
3. Brush with olive oil. Sprinkle with salt or any seasoning you desire.
Air fry at 270°F for 12 to 15 minutes or until golden brown and crispy.
4. Cool in a cooling rack and repeat with remaining zucchini coins.

Nutritional Value (Amount per Serving):

Calories: 117; Fat: 10.96; Carb: 0; Protein: 4.62

Air Fryer Crispy Artichokes

Prep Time: 3 Mins   Cook Time: 12 Mins   Serves: 2

Ingredients:

- ½ cup all purpose flour
- 1 large egg
- 1 Tbsp water
- ¼ tsp garlic powder
- ¼ teaspoon onion powder
- ¼ teaspoon dried thyme
- 1 Tbsp grated Parmesan cheese
- ½ cup regular or Italian bread crumbs
- ½ cup Panko Japanese style bread crumbs

- ⅛ teaspoon salt
- 1 can halved or quartered artichokes hearts in water, drained

Directions:

1. Lightly spray the inside of the air fryer basket with oil spray. Set the basket aside.
2. Drain the canned artichoke hearts and pat dry with paper towels, pressing carefully to remove as much water as possible. Set the artichoke hearts aside.
3. In a shallow bowl add flour, set aside. In a second bowl, add 1 egg plus 1 Tbsp water and whisk completely, set aside. In the 3rd bowl add garlic powder, onion powder, thyme, Parmesan cheese, bread crumbs, panko bread crumbs, and salt. Whisk to combine completely, set aside.
4. Taking a few artichoke hearts at a time, add them to the flour and toss to coat, then place into the egg and toss to coat. Add the egg coated artichokes to the bread crumb mixture and toss to coat. Press the artichokes into the bread crumb mixture a bit to make sure the coating sticks. Place the artichokes into the air fryer basket as you coat them. Repeat until all the artichoke hearts are coated and placed into the air fryer. Lightly spray the tops of them with oil spray.
5. Close the air fryer. Set at 375 degrees F for 6 minutes. Open the air fryer, flip the artichokes carefully, spray the tops with oil spray, then close and cook 2-3 more minutes.
6. Remove the artichokes and then serve alongside your favorite dipping sauce!

Nutritional Value (Amount per Serving):

Calories: 272; Fat: 4.64; Carb: 33.7; Protein: 22.98

Crispy Air Fryer Oyster Mushrooms

Prep Time: 15 Mins   Cook Time: 25 Mins   Serves: 4

Ingredients:

- 7 oz oyster mushrooms cleaned
- ⅓ cup almond milk unsweetened and unflavored (or other kinds of milk)
- ½ teaspoon apple cider vinegar
- ½ teaspoon hot sauce
- ¾ cup all purpose flour   or wholemeal flour/almond flour/gluten-free blend
- 2 tablespoons cornstarch
- 1 teaspoon salt
- ¾ teaspoon onion powder

- ¾ teaspoon garlic powder
- ¾ teaspoon dried oregano
- ¾ teaspoon dried basil
- ¾ teaspoon paprika powder
- ½ teaspoon cracked pepper

Directions:

1. In a shallow bowl, mix together all wet ingredients. Set aside.
2. In a separate bowl, combine all ingredients needed for the coating.
3. Dip a piece of oyster mushroom in the milk mixture, shaking off excess. Then, coat it in the flour mixture and shake off extra. Repeat for the remaining mushrooms.
4. Lightly coat the bottom of the air fryer basket with oil, and place mushrooms in one layer without overlapping. (Hence, you might need to cook them in batches)

Spray a layer of oil on the mushrooms, then bake them at 350°F for 8-12 minutes, flipping and spraying on more oil halfway through.

5. Serve them with dipping sauce of choice, and enjoy!

Nutritional Value (Amount per Serving):

Calories: 135; Fat: 0.77; Carb: 28.24; Protein: 4.57

Chapter 7: Vegetables and Salads

Air Fryer Leeks

Prep Time: 10 Mins   Cook Time: 20 Mins   Serves: 2

Ingredients:

- 2 leeks only the white and light green parts
- 1 Tablespoon olive oil
- ¼ teaspoon dried thyme leaves
- ¼ teaspoon salt

Directions:

1. Chop the dark green section off of the leeks so that you' only have the light green and white sections remaining. Discard the dark green section.
2. Chop the white and light green parts of the leeks into rounds about ½ inch thick. Place in a bowl of water.
3. Swish the leeks around in the bowl of water, separating any layers as needed to remove the dirt in between layers. Rinse the leeks, then dry on paper towels.
4. Add leeks to a bowl, then add the olive oil, thyme, and salt. Toss to combine.
5. Place in the air fryer and air fry for 7-10 minutes at 400 degrees F, tossing every few minutes, until leeks are cooked to your desired level of doneness.
6. Remove from air fryer and enjoy as desired.

Nutritional Value (Amount per Serving):

Calories: 114; Fat: 7.03; Carb: 12.69; Protein: 1.35

Air Fryer Stuffed Zucchini Blossoms

Prep Time: 10 Mins   Cook Time: 22 Mins   Serves: 1

Ingredients:

- 4 Zucchini (or squash) flowers
- ½ cup ricotta
- 2 teaspoons fresh basil chopped
- ½ teaspoon lemon zest
- salt
- pepper
- 1 egg white
- ¼ cup all purpose flour
- olive oil spray

Directions:

1. Take your zucchini flowers and gently remove the inner parts and any outer green parts. Rinse gently under water.
2. Add your ricotta, chopped basil, lemon zest, and a touch of salt and pepper to a medium bowl. Stir to combine.
3. Take each zucchini flower and place a small amount of ricotta filling in the

center, pressing the leaves back together to seal, and slightly twisting the top to seal.
4. Add your egg white (slightly beaten) to one bowl and flour to a separate bowl.
5. Dip each zucchini flower in the egg white, then gently in the flour, gently shaking off any excess.
6. Lightly spray each zucchini flower with olive oil spray, then place in the air fryer basket.
7. Air fry at 380 degrees F for 12 minutes, flipping halfway and lightly spraying the other side with oil when flipping.
8. Remove from air fryer and enjoy. Serve with marinara, a squeeze of lemon juice, or any other way you prefer.

Nutritional Value (Amount per Serving):

Calories: 614; Fat: 30.88; Carb: 61.41; Protein: 21.78

Air Fryer Fennel

Prep Time: 5 Mins   Cook Time: 20 Mins   Serves: 2

Ingredients:

- 1 fennel bulb
- 1 Tablespoon olive oil
- salt
- black pepper

Directions:

1. Take your fennel and slice off any stalks and fronds, if needed.
2. Slice the fennel bulb into 8 wedges. Add to a large bowl.
3. Add the olive oil, and a sprinkling of salt and pepper to the bowl. Gently toss to combine.
Add the fennel wedges in a single layer in the air fryer basket. Air fry at 380°F for 15 minutes, flipping halfway through the cooking time.
4. Remove from the air fryer and serve as desired!

Nutritional Value (Amount per Serving):

Calories: 99; Fat: 7.02; Carb: 9.28; Protein: 1.57

Air Fried Panzanella Salad

Prep Time: 5 Mins   Cook Time: 12 Mins   Serves: 2

Ingredients:

- 2 slices Sourdough
- 2 tsp Olive Oil
- 1 tsp Garlic Powder
- 10-12 Cherry Tomatoes

- 2 Tomatoes
- 4 oz Iceberg Lettuce
- 1 oz Pine Nuts
- 6-10 pearls Mozzarella
- 3-4 leaves Basil
- ½ squeeze of Lemon Juice

Directions:

1. Cut the two slices of bread and season with the olive oil and garlic powder.
2. In a bowl mix the veggie and mozzarella. Season with lemon juice and a bit of olive oil. Salt to taste

Air Fry the bread for 7 minutes at 360°F. Sprinkle on top of the salad.

Nutritional Value (Amount per Serving):

Calories: 438; Fat: 24.21; Carb: 20.78; Protein: 39.53

25 Minutes Sweet & Sticky Air Fryer Eggplant

Prep Time: 5 Mins   Cook Time: 23 Mins   Serves: 4

Ingredients:

- 1 large eggplant, cut in chunks or cubes
- 5 tablespoons agave nectar, divided (honey or maple syrup works too)
- 4 tablespoons sesame oil, divided
- 1/2 teaspoon kosher salt
- 1 tablespoon tamari or soy sauce
- 1/2 teaspoon hot sauce
- 1 scallion, chopped
- sprinkle of white sesame seeds for garnish

Directions:

Preheat your air fryer to 400°F.

1. Cut the eggplant into 2 inch pieces that are about 1/2 inch thick. I did a combo of triangles and rectangles.
2. Place the eggplant in a large bowl and toss with 3 tablespoons agave nectar and 3 tablespoons sesame oil.
3. Arrange the eggplant pieces in your air fryer basket or tray in a single layer. Make sure they aren't touching. Sprinkle with salt.
4. Place the basket or tray into a preheated air fryer and air fry for 8 minutes.
5. While the eggplant is air frying, whisk together the sauce with the remaining 2 tablespoons agave nectar, 1 tablespoon sesame oil, soy sauce, and hot sauce.
6. After the 8 minutes, if you are using trays, switch the trays so the eggplant cooks evenly. Brush the eggplant with the sauce. Air fry for another 5 minutes.
7. After the 5 minutes, use tongs to flip the eggplant and brush the other side with the sauce.

8. Air fry for another 3 – 5 minutes until caramelized and golden-medium brown.
9. Transfer to a plate or bowl and garnish with scallions and sesame seeds.

Nutritional Value (Amount per Serving):

Calories: 469; Fat: 36.83; Carb: 29.75; Protein: 9.57

Air Fryer Avocado Fries

Prep Time: 10 Mins   Cook Time: 30 Mins   Serves: 6

Ingredients:

- 3 medium avocados
- 1/2 cup all purpose flour
- 1/2 tsp kosher salt
- 1/2 tsp black pepper
- 1/4 tsp paprika
- 1 cup panko breadcrumbs
- 1/2 cup everything bagel seasoning
- 2 large eggs
- splash of water
- cooking spray

Directions:

6. Preheat air fryer to 400°F. Line a plate with wax paper and set aside, near the air fryer.
7. Slice avocados in half, lengthwise, removing the pit. Peel the skin off the avocado and slice each avocado half lengthwise into roughly 1/2" thick slices.
8. Get out 3 shallow bowls. To the first one, add flour, 1/2 tsp black pepper, 1/2 tsp salt, and 1/4 tsp paprika. Stir with a fork until combined.
9. In the second bowl, add 2 eggs and splash of water and whisk. In the third bowl, add the panko and the everything bagel seasoning. Stir with a fork to combine.
10. Coat the avocado slices, one at a time, in the flour mixture, then in the eggs, then in the panko mixture. Set aside on a plate and repeat with remaining slices.
11. Spray basket of air fryer with nonstick spray to prevent any sticking.
12. Add breaded avocado slices in a single layer to the bottom of the air fryer basket, making sure they're not touching each other. You'll likely have to cook the avocado slices in batches. Lightly spray with a canola oil cooking spray, then cook for 4 minutes.
13. Open air fryer, turn over avocado slices, spray with cooking spray, then cook for another 2-3 minutes, or until golden and crunchy.
14. Set cooked avocado fries on a plate and repeat with any remaining avocado slices.
15. Serve immediately, served with desired dipping sauce.

Nutritional Value (Amount per Serving):

Calories: 254; Fat: 16.72; Carb: 23.82; Protein: 5.37

Easy Air Fryer Green Beans

Prep Time: 2 Mins   Cook Time: 8 Mins   Serves: 4

Ingredients:

- 1 pound green beans
- cooking spray
- salt to taste

Directions:

1. Preheat the air fryer to 400 degrees F.
2. Add the green beans to a bowl and spray with some low-calorie spray and the best salt ever and combine.
3. Place the beans into the air fryer basket and cook for 6-8 minutes, turning a couple of times during cooking so that they brown evenly.
4. Remove and serve topped with some extra salt and chopped herbs if you like.

Nutritional Value (Amount per Serving):

Calories: 26; Fat: 0.58; Carb: 4.91; Protein: 1.27

Air Fryer Butternut Squash Fries

Prep Time: 5 Mins   Cook Time: 17 Mins   Serves: 4

Ingredients:

- 3 cups butternut squash peeled and cut into 1-inch cubes
- 1 tbsp olive oil
- 1 tsp dried oregano
- 1/2 tsp smoked paprika
- salt to taste

Directions:

Preheat Air Fryer to 400°F.

1. Combine all ingredients in a bowl and toss to make sure squash is well coated.
2. Add the butternut squash fries to the air fryer basket, making sure they are in a single layer. You may need to cook them in batches, depending on the size of your air fryer.
3. Cook for 15-20 mins, making sure to turn every 5 mins. You can cook for a longer time if you want the edges to caramelize.

Nutritional Value (Amount per Serving):

Calories: 45; Fat: 3.58; Carb: 3.17; Protein: 1.09

Air Fryer Zucchini Fries

Prep Time: 10 Mins   Cook Time: 20 Mins   Serves: 4

Ingredients:

- 2 zucchinis (courgettes) cut into fries that are about ½ inch thick
- 2/3 cup almond flour
- 1/4 cup Parmesan cheese
- 1 tsp smoked paprika
- salt
- olive oil spray

Directions:

Preheat air fryer to 400°F.
1. Combine the almond flour, Parmesan cheese, smoked paprika and salt in a medium bowl.
2. Place zucchini fries in another bowl and spray with olive oil spray.
3. Dip zucchini fries into the Parmesan cheese mixture, making sure all sides are well coated.
4. Place fries in a single layer inside the air fryer basket.
5. Cook for 7-10 mins until golden and crispy.
6. Remove from air fryer and serve.

Nutritional Value (Amount per Serving):

Calories: 76; Fat: 5.63; Carb: 4.27; Protein: 3.09

Easy Air Fryer Fried Pickles

Prep Time: 5 Mins   Cook Time: 15 Mins   Serves: 3

Ingredients:

- 2 cups sliced pickles
- 1 cup buttermilk mixed with a dash of Franks hot seasoning (optional)
- 1 cup breadcrumbs
- ¼ cup grated Parmesan
- 1 teaspoon oregano
- ⅓ teaspoon smoked paprika
- ¼ teaspoon garlic powder

Directions:

1. Preheat the Air Fryer to 400 degrees F.
2. Pat the pickles dry.
3. Put seasoned buttermilk in a bowl.
4. Mix together breadcrumbs, cheese and seasonings in another bowl.

5. Working quickly dip pickles in buttermilk mix, shake to drip off excess buttermilk, dredge both sides of the pickle in the seasoned breadcrumb mixture and add to basket.
6. Keep working quickly to fill the basket, insert the basket into the Air Fryer and fry for 8-10 minutes.
7. About 3 minutes before they're done, lightly spray the pickles with spray oil so that the breadcrumbs can crisp up and become golden brown.
8. Repeat by breading the rest of the pickles and continuing to fry in batches until finished.

Nutritional Value (Amount per Serving):

Calories: 53; Fat: 0.59; Carb: 8.15; Protein: 3.84

Air Fryer Frozen Vegetables

Prep Time: 1 Mins   Cook Time: 10 Mins   Serves: 4

Ingredients:

- 12 ounces frozen carrots
- 12 ounces frozen green beans
- oil or calorie-controlled cooking spray
- garlic salt to taste
- dry seasoning optional and to taste

Directions:

Preheat Air fryer to 400°F.
1. Mix frozen beans or frozen carrots with oil and garlic salt and place them into the air fryer basket.
2. Air fry for 8-11 minutes or until sizzling turning halfway through.
3. If you want them browned you can air fry for a couple more minutes.

Nutritional Value (Amount per Serving):

Calories: 176; Fat: 0.63; Carb: 33.23; Protein: 3.77

Slow Roasted Grape and Cherry Tomatoes

Prep Time: 15 Mins   Cook Time: 1 Hour 15 Mins   Serves: 4

Ingredients:

- 2 pounds grape and cherry tomatoes cut in half lengthwise
- 2 tablespoons olive oil
- 4-8 garlic cloves whole and unpeeled
- salt to taste

Directions:

Preheat Air Fryer to 250°F.

1. Halve the tomatoes, add them to a mixing bowl and mix in the olive oil, garlic and salt. Add them to the Air Fryer basket with the cut side up.
2. Cook for 1 hour 15 minutes (according to the size of your tomatoes), checking around 40 minutes and again at 60 minutes. If they need a little more time, cook in additional 15-minute increments.
3. Let cool before serving or storing.

Nutritional Value (Amount per Serving):

Calories: 209; Fat: 7.23; Carb: 37.8; Protein: 2.69

Air Fryer Beets

Prep Time: 5 Mins   Cook Time: 23 Mins   Serves: 4

Ingredients:

- 1 pound beets peeled and cut into one-inch pieces
- 1 tablespoon olive oil
- 1 tablespoon orange juice
- salt to taste
- dill fronds, chopped

Directions:

1. Peel the beets and cut them into one-inch cubes.
2. Combine with the olive oil and orange juice in a mixing bowl.
Preheat the air fryer to 400°F.
3. Place beets in the air fryer basket and cook for16-18 minutes, shaking a couple of times.
4. Transfer to a plate, taste and adjust seasonings, then top with dill (if desired).

Nutritional Value (Amount per Serving):

Calories: 81; Fat: 3.57; Carb: 11.29; Protein: 1.85

Air Fryer Kale Chips

Prep Time: 5 Mins   Cook Time: 10 Mins   Serves: 4

Ingredients:

- 1 bunch kale
- salt to taste
- 1 spritz oil or calorie-controlled cooking spray (optional)

Directions:

Preheat your air fryer to 375°F.
1. Wash, dry and tear the kale.
2. Add the kale to the air fryer basket, filling about halfway.
3. Spritz with oil and sprinkle with salt.
4. Air fry in batches for 4-6 minutes, shaking a couple of times during cooking.
5. Kale chips can burn quickly, so it's important to check it frequently, beginning at the 3-minute mark.

Nutritional Value (Amount per Serving):

Calories: 10; Fat: 0.6; Carb: 0.2; Protein: 3

Air Fryer Frozen Broccoli

Prep Time: 1 Mins   Cook Time: 12 Mins   Serves: 4

Ingredients:

- 1 pound frozen broccoli
- 2 teaspoons oil or calorie-controlled cooking spray
- ½ teaspoon garlic powder or to taste
- salt to taste

Directions:

Preheat Air fryer to 400°F.
1. Mix frozen broccoli with oil and garlic, powder, and salt and place into the air fryer basket.
2. Air fry for 8-14 minutes or until sizzling and browning at the edges, turning halfway through.
3. If you want it crispier, you can air fry for a couple more minutes, but keep an eye on it so it doesn't burn.

Nutritional Value (Amount per Serving):

Calories: 35; Fat: 0.51; Carb: 6.39; Protein: 3.54

Chapter 8: Beans and Grains

Air Dryer Green Beans

Prep Time: 5 Mins   Cook Time: 15 Mins   Serves: 2

Ingredients:

- 8 ounces fresh green beans, trimmed (½ pound)
- 2 cloves garlic, minced
- 1 Tablespoon olive oil
- salt and pepper, to taste
- fresh lemon juice, for serving

Directions:

1. In a large mixing bowl, toss the green beans and garlic with the olive oil and salt and pepper, to taste, so that everything is well coated.
2. Transfer the mixture to the basket or tray of an air fryer. Air fry at 375°F for 8 to 10 minutes, or until the green beans reach your desired level of doneness, shaking or tossing halfway through.
3. Transfer the green beans to a serving plate. Squeeze fresh lemon juice over them and serve warm or at room temperature.

Nutritional Value (Amount per Serving):

Calories: 104; Fat: 7.42; Carb: 9.78; Protein: 1.88

Air Fryer Bread

Prep Time: 10 Mins   Cook Time: 45 Mins   Serves: 16

Ingredients:

- ½ cup Greek yogurt full-fat
- 4 large eggs
- 2 tbsp apple cider vinegar
- 1 cup almond flour blanched
- 2 tbsp coconut flour
- 2 tbsp oat fiber
- 2 tbsp psyllium husk powder
- 1 tbsp baking powder
- 1 tsp salt
- ½ cup sunflower seeds optional, or other seeds (use unsalted)

Directions:

1. In a large bowl, whisk together yogurt, eggs, and apple cider vinegar. Set aside.
2. In a medium bowl, whisk together all remaining ingredients, except seeds (if using). Add dry ingredients to wet ingredients and stir until well combined.

Let rest for 5 minutes, then stir in seeds if desired.

3. Shape dough on a piece of parchment paper. To shape, wet your hands, this will prevent the dough from sticking to your fingers. I went for a rectangular shape of about 7"x4", but you can also make an oval loaf. Cut around the parchment paper, so that it's only slightly largen than the loaf and place the bread on the parchment in the lowest tray of your Air Fryer basket.

Bake at 340°F for 35 minutes, flipping the bread upside down midway through. Be careful when you do that, as the bread will be hot. I use a clean kitchen towel for flipping. Enjoy with your favourite toppings!

Nutritional Value (Amount per Serving):

Calories: 97; Fat: 8.2; Carb: 4.01; Protein: 3.75

Air Fried Kidney Beans

Prep Time: 5 Mins   Cook Time: 30 Mins   Serves: 2-3

Ingredients:

- 1 can red kidney bean
- 1 tsp oil
- Seasoning of choice

Directions:

1. Rinse and dry the beans well.
2. Preheat the air fryer.
3. Mix seasoning, oil, and beans and mix well.Add to the air fryer basket, and air fry it for 15-18 minutes at 375°F . Shake the basket a few times.
4. Once done, remove from the basket and enjoy anytime.

Nutritional Value (Amount per Serving):

Calories: 134; Fat: 2.02; Carb: 22.11; Protein: 7.63

Roasted Lupini Beans in the Air Fryer

Prep Time: 5 Mins   Cook Time: 15 Mins   Serves: 8

Ingredients:

- 1 can (19oz) Lupini beans rinse and drain
- Juice of 1 lime
- 1 teaspoon chili powder
- 1 teaspoon olive oil
- Salt and Pepper to taste

Directions:

1. Rinse and drain the Lupini bean.

2. Place the Lupini in a medium bowl and add the juice of one lime, chili powder, olive oil, and salt, pepper to taste. Mix well to combine everything.
3. Place the Lupini beans in the basket of the air fryer. Close the air fryer, select 380°F and cook 10 minutes.
4. Mix halfway through cooking (after 5 minutes).
5. Served as a snack.

Nutritional Value (Amount per Serving):

Calories: 47; Fat: 0.94; Carb: 7.86; Protein: 2.45

Crispy Roasted White Beans

Prep Time: 10 Mins   Cook Time: 40 Mins   Serves: 3

Ingredients:

- 1 (15 oz) can white beans, such as cannellini or navy
- 1 tablespoon oil
- salt and pepper - to taste
- spice blends like harissa, za'atar, curry, or chili powder

Directions:

1. Preheat air fryer to 400°F.
2. Rinse and drain the beans, then spread them out on a large tea towel or paper towels and pat dry. If you accidentally smash some of the beans that's okay! We actually enjoy the variety of having some intact and some smashed beans.
3. Spread the beans out on a large plate and gently toss with the oil and your choice of seasoning. Taste a few beans to make sure they're well-seasoned. Transfer to the air fryer basket, spreading them out in a single layer.
4. Roast in the air fryer for about 12 minutes. Shake the pan or gently stir the beans at the halfway mark.
5. Keep a close eye on the beans as they roast. The beans are ready when golden brown and crispy on the outside, but still tender on the inside. Serve and enjoy!

Nutritional Value (Amount per Serving):

Calories: 278; Fat: 5.52; Carb: 43.33; Protein: 2.39

Roasted Fava Beans

Prep Time: 10 Mins   Cook Time: 30 Mins   Serves: 4

Ingredients:

- 2 cups shelled fava beans

- ½ tablespoon extra virgin olive oil
- ¼ teaspoon sea salt kosher salt is also fine
- ⅛ teaspoon ground black pepper

Directions:

1. Wash and shell your broad beans. The pods are easy to peel and you can put the beans into a mixing bowl as you go. Rinse the beans with cold water and pat them dry with a paper towel.
2. To prepare the fava beans, add the shelled fava bean seeds to a bowl. Combine the minced garlic and olive oil. Add this mixture to the beans along with kosher salt and ground black pepper. Toss to coat all of the beans.

Preheat your air fryer to 375°F.

3. Place the seasoned fava beans in the air fryer basket. Be sure they are spread out and don't overlap too much. The air needs to circulate around the beans so they cook evenly.
4. Air fry the beans for 7 minutes, then stir the beans to cook the other side.
5. Air fry an additional 5-7 minutes.
6. Serve the cooked beans hot.

Nutritional Value (Amount per Serving):

Calories: 63; Fat: 1.21; Carb: 11.25; Protein: 5.03

Crispy Roasted Lentils

Prep Time: 5 Mins   Cook Time: 25 Mins   Serves: 4

Ingredients:

- 2 cups cooked lentils canned or from scratch cooked lentils. Drained and rinsed if using canned lentils.
- 2 tablespoons olive oil
- 1 teaspoon chipotle paste or 1 & ½ teaspoons adobo sauce from a can or 3/4 teaspoon dried chipotle powder

Directions:

Preheat air fryer to 400°F.

1. Combine lentils with oil and chipotle in a medium bowl, and toss gently to combine. Spread coated lentils on a small sheet of aluminum foil, and fold up the sides of the foil to create a tray. You may need to cook these in batches depending on how large your air fryer is.

Roast at 400°F until lightly crisp, about 15 minutes, stirring halfway through.

Nutritional Value (Amount per Serving):

Calories: 273; Fat: 12.47; Carb: 31.64; Protein: 10.03

Crispy Air Fryer Parmesan Edamame

Prep Time: 5 Mins   Cook Time: 15 Mins   Serves: 2

Ingredients:

- 2.5 cups shelled edamame beans
- 1-2 tbsp olive oil
- 1/2 tbsp garlic powder
- 1/3 cup Parmesan cheese

Directions:

1. Thaw your edamame beans by soaking it for up to 5 minutes in water. Drain and pat dry.
2. Toss the edamame beans in olive oil, garlic powder, and and Parmesan cheese.
3. Add the edamame to the air fryer basket and set the air fryer to 400F and air fry for 8-10 minutes. Making sure to shake the basket at least once during the cooking cycle.

Optional: At the end of the cooking cycle (last 2 minutes), I like to lower the heat to 350°F and add another sprinkling of Parmesan cheese – just became who doesn't like more Parmesan!?

4. Let cool and serve.

Nutritional Value (Amount per Serving):

Calories: 209; Fat: 15.64; Carb: 12.34; Protein: 7.24

Air Fryer Cannellini Beans

Prep Time: 5 Mins   Cook Time: 25 Mins   Serves: 6

Ingredients:

- 15 ounces cannellini beans
- 2 teaspoons olive oil
- 1 teaspoon seasoning, any type

Directions:

1. Drain the cannellini beans using a colander, then run cold water over the beans. Then lay them out on a paper towel or kitchen towel, and leave them for about 10 minutes until they are dried.
2. Add your cannellini beans to a large bowl, add the oil and seasoning, and toss well to coat.
3. Pour the beans into the air fryer basket, set the temperature to 400 degrees F, and cook for 12 to 15 minutes, shaking the basket several times during the cooking process. Remove when the beans are crispy!

Nutritional Value (Amount per Serving):

Calories: 30; Fat: 1.83; Carb: 3.34; Protein: 0.82

Air Fryer Butter Beans

Prep Time: 3 Mins   Cook Time: 15 Mins   Serves: 4

Ingredients:

- 15.5 oz butter beans, 1 can
- 1 tbsp olive oil
- 1 tsp garlic powder
- 1 tsp onion powder
- ½ tsp cumin powder
- kosher salt

Directions:

1. Preheat your air fryer to 370 degrees Fahrenheit.
2. Drain your butter beans and lay them out on a sheet of paper towel, and pat them dry.
3. In a large bowl, toss your beans with olive oil, spices, and salt to taste.
4. Spread your beans in a single layer in the air fryer basket and cook for 10-15 minutes (tossing them once halfway through the cooking time.)
5. After ten minutes, check your beans. Cook for another 5 minutes if you like them extra crispy.

Nutritional Value (Amount per Serving):

Calories: 823; Fat: 92.55; Carb: 1.23; Protein: 1.17

Air Fryer Mung Beans

Prep Time: 12 Hours   Cook Time: 12 Hrs 20 Mins   Serves: 2

Ingredients:

- ½ cup mung beans raw whole moong
- water
- salt as per taste
- 2 teaspoon oil, 1 teaspoon for each batch
- 1 teaspoon chat masala

Directions:

1. Soak ½ cup whole moong, at least 12 hours or 1 day, change water 2-3 times.
2. Once the moong beans have been soaked well, drain the excess water.
3. Boil water. Cook the green moong for 8-10 minutes in boiling water or until its soft. Allow it to cool for some time

Preheat the air fryer at 355°F for 10 minutes. Toss the green moong in 1 teaspoon oil.

4. Spread half the moong on crisping tray / parchment paper .
Cook for 8 -10 mins at 355°F and mix 2-3 times in between
5. Once done, take it outside,keep it aside. Repeat for remaining mung beans.
6. Add the spices, mix well. Store it in air tight container once it cools.

Nutritional Value (Amount per Serving):

Calories: 56; Fat: 4.67; Carb: 3.04; Protein: 1.26

Crispy Parmesan Air Fryer Green Bean

Prep Time: 15 Mins   Cook Time: 30 Mins   Serves: 1

Ingredients:

- 1/4 cup flour
- 2 eggs, beaten
- 1/2 cup grated Parmesan
- 1 cup panko bread crumbs
- 1 lb green and yellow beans
- salt and pepper, to taste

Directions:

1. Wash the green and yellow beans, yet don't dry them. If they are a little wet the flour will stick to them better.
2. Place the flour in a medium bowl.
3. Place the beaten eggs in the second medium bowl
4. And finally, combine the panko breadcrumbs and grated Parmesan in a third medium bowl.
5. Take one bean at a time, first dip it the flour, followed by the eggs, and finally dip in the panko bread mixture.
6. Repeat with the rest of the green and yellow beans.
7. Place the beans in a single layer in the basket of the air fryer. You will have to do 2 batches.
Cook at 380°F for 10 minutes, Stir halfway through cooking.
8. Serve immediately with a dipping sauce if desired.

Nutritional Value (Amount per Serving):

Calories: 937; Fat: 33.15; Carb: 106.4; Protein: 53.59

Crunchy Roasted Peas

Prep Time: 5 Mins   Cook Time: 25 Mins   Serves: 1

Ingredients:

- 1 cup Frozen Peas
- 1 teaspoon Olive Oil
- 1 teaspoon Garlic Powder
- Salt, to taste

Directions:

1. Defrost peas, then dry them with a clean kitchen towel or paper towel. Place them in a bowl and mix together with olive oil, garlic powder and salt.

Pour peas into the air fryer basket and cook on 350°F for approximately 15 minutes. You'll need to shake the basket every few minutes to ensure even cooking and check in on your peas regularly. They're ready when they are nice and crispy.

Nutritional Value (Amount per Serving):

Calories: 111; Fat: 4.95; Carb: 12.62; Protein: 4.55

Crispy Roasted Black Beans

Prep Time: 5 Mins   Cook Time: 45 Mins   Serves: 4

Ingredients:

- 1 ½ cups cooked black beans or a 15 oz can
- 1 tablespoon olive oil or other neutral-tasting oil
- ¼ teaspoon garlic powder
- ¼ teaspoon salt
- generous pinch of black pepper

Directions:

Preheat air fryer to 400°F.

1. Drain your beans, then gently dry them using a napkin or some kitchen towels.
2. Transfer black beans to a large bowl and add in all seasonings. Toss until seasonings are well distributed.
3. Spread them in one layer in your air fryer. Cook at 400F for 10-12 minutes, or until they are crispy and nicely browned.

Nutritional Value (Amount per Serving):

Calories: 31; Fat: 1.69; Carb: 3.17; Protein: 0.91

Rice and Lentil Pilaf

Prep Time: 20 Mins   Cook Time: 40 Mins   Serves: 4

Ingredients:

- 1 cup white or brown rice
- 1/2 cup green or brown lentils
- 1/4 cup olive oil
- 1 small onion, finely chopped
- 2 cloves garlic, minced
- 1 teaspoon ground cumin

- 1 teaspoon ground coriander
- 1/2 teaspoon ground turmeric
- 2 cups vegetable broth
- 1/4 cup chopped fresh parsley
- 1/4 cup chopped fresh mint
- Salt and pepper to taste
- Lemon wedges for serving

Directions:

1. Preheat your air fryer to 375°F.
2. Rinse the rice and lentils separately. In a saucepan, heat 2 tablespoons of olive oil. Add the chopped onion and minced garlic and sauté until they're soft and translucent.
3. Stir in the ground cumin, ground coriander, and ground turmeric. Cook for a minute to toast the spices.
4. Add the rice and lentils to the saucepan. Stir them into the spiced onion mixture.
5. Pour in the vegetable broth. Bring to a boil, then reduce the heat, cover, and simmer for about 15-20 minutes.
6. Once the rice and lentils are cooked, fluff them with a fork. Season with salt and pepper, and add the remaining olive oil, fresh parsley, and fresh mint. Mix well.
7. Transfer the rice and lentil pilaf to an air fryer-safe dish. Lightly spray the top with olive oil cooking spray.
8. Place the dish in the air fryer. Air fry at 375°F for about 10 minutes, or until the top becomes slightly crispy.
9. Once the pilaf is done, remove it from the air fryer and serve with lemon wedges!

Nutritional Value (Amount per Serving):

Calories: 186; Fat: 14.94; Carb: 10.22; Protein: 4.36

Chapter 9: Desserts

Air Fryer Pineapple

Prep Time: 10 Mins   Cook Time: 30 Mins   Serves: 4

Ingredients:

- 1 fresh pineapple, peeled, cored, and sliced, at room temperature (about 8 slices)
- 1 tablespoon coconut oil, melted
- 2 tablespoons brown sugar (or coconut sugar)
- 1/2 teaspoon ground cinnamon
- 1 cup prepared whipped cream (use a dairy-free version for vegan diets) (optional)

Directions:

1. Place the pineapple slices in a medium mixing bowl and set aside.
2. Then, in a small bowl, combine the coconut oil, brown sugar, and cinnamon. Stir gently to combine.
3. Pour the coconut oil mixture over the pineapple slices. And stir gently to coat the pineapple
4. Lay the pineapple slices in your air fryer basket, trying to keep the slices from touching each other.
5. Set the temperature of your air fryer to 375 degrees F for 8 minutes.
6. Use tongs to flip the slices and cook for an additional 6-8 minutes, or until the pineapple slices start to brown and caramelize.
7. Serve immediately, with a dollop of whipped cream on top.

Nutritional Value (Amount per Serving):

Calories: 160; Fat: 15; Carb: 5.77; Protein: 1.68

Air Fryer Baked Apples with Oats

Prep Time: 10 Mins   Cook Time: 35 Mins   Serves: 6

Ingredients:

- Non-stick cooking spray
- 3 Red or green apples
- 1/3 cup rolled oats (gluten-free, if necessary)
- 1 tablespoon coconut oil, melted
- 3 tablespoons brown sugar or coconut sugar
- 1/4 teaspoon ground cinnamon

Directions:

1. Spray the inside of your air fryer basket with non-stick cooking spray and set aside.

2. Wash your apples and cut them in half. Use a spoon or melon baller to scoop out the seeds and the core of each half of the apple

3. Lay the apples skin side down in the basket of your air fryer. If the apples don't want to lay flat, you can slice a tiny amount of the skin off to help them balance. Bake them for 10 minutes at 350°F to soften.

4. While the apples are baking, combine the oats, coconut oil, sugar, and cinnamon in a small bowl. Stir to combine.

5. After the 10 minutes are up, open the air fryer basket. Use a spoon to divide the oat mixture between the apples (about 1 ½ tablespoons per apple half).

6. Close the air fryer and cook the apples for an additional 10 minutes.

7. Let the apples cool for 5 minutes before serving.

Nutritional Value (Amount per Serving):

Calories: 96; Fat: 2.83; Carb: 20.08; Protein: 1.14

Air Fryer Banana Chips with Cinnamon

Prep Time: 5 Mins   Cook Time: 22 Mins   Serves: 4

Ingredients:

- Nonstick cooking spray
- 2 bananas (not overly ripe)
- 2 teaspoons olive oil or your favorite cooking oil
- 1/4 teaspoon ground cinnamon
- 1 tablespoon brown sugar or coconut sugar

Directions:

1. Spray the bottom of your air fryer basket liberally with nonstick cooking spray and set aside.

2. Remove the bananas from their skins and slice the bananas thinly (about ¼-inch thick). Try to slice the bananas as uniformly as possible so they will cook evenly.

3. Place the sliced bananas in a medium mixing bowl. Add the oil, cinnamon, and sugar. Toss gently to combine.

4. Transfer the bananas to your air fryer basket and try to spread them out. It is okay if they overlap slightly, but they should mostly be in a single layer. Depending on the size of your air fryer, you many need to bake them in two batches.

5. Set the temperature to 350°F for 10 minutes. Use tongs to turn the banana chips over and cook for an additional 7-10 minutes, or until they have started to brown and crisp up. Be careful to not let them burn.

6. Transfer the banana chips to a serving plate to cool before serving. The banana chips will crisp up as they cool.

Nutritional Value (Amount per Serving):

Calories: 191; Fat: 1.94; Carb: 46.2; Protein: 1.96

Air Fryer Granola

Prep Time: 10 Mins   Cook Time: 25 Mins   Serves: 5

Ingredients:

- 1 cup rolled oats (use gluten-free, if necessary)
- 1/4 chopped almonds
- 1/4 pumpkin seeds
- 2 tablespoons raisins
- 1/4 teaspoon sea salt
- 3 tablespoons maple syrup
- 3 tablespoons coconut oil, melted

Directions:

1. In a medium bowl, combine the oats, almonds, pumpkin seeds, raisins, sea salt, maple syrup, and coconut oil. Stir to combine.
2. Line the basket of your air fryer with parchment paper to prevent the granola from falling through the basket.
3. Pour the granola into the basket on top of the parchment paper. Set the temperature to 350°F for 12 minutes, stopping once to open the basket and gently stir the ingredients.
4. When the granola is done cooking, the oats will have started to turn a golden brown.
5. Carefully remove the parchment paper from the air fryer basket and pour the granola into a glass storage jar or bowl.
6. Let it cool slightly before serving.

Nutritional Value (Amount per Serving):

Calories: 149; Fat: 12.41; Carb: 21.; Protein: 3.28

Peaches With Oat Crumble

Prep Time: 5 Mins   Cook Time: 25 Mins   Serves: 8

Ingredients:

- 4 ripe yellow peaches, pitted
- 1 cup old-fashioned rolled oats
- 1/2 cup oat flour or spelt flour
- 3 tablespoons pure maple syrup
- 3 tablespoons melted coconut oil
- 1 teaspoon vanilla extract

- 1 teaspoon ground cinnamon
- Pinch of salt

Directions:

1. Cut the peaches in half and carefully remove the pit. Place the peach, cut-side up on a piece of baking paper. Dust each with cinnamon; set aside.
2. Mix together the oats, cinnamon, vanilla, oil and maple syrup in a bowl.
3. Divide the oat topping evenly over the peaches.
   Add peaches on the baking paper to the air fryer basket and cook at 320°F for 15-20 minutes or until golden. Cooking at a low heat helps prevent the topping from browning too early.
4. If desired, top servings with a scoop of ice cream or yogurt.

Nutritional Value (Amount per Serving):

Calories: 218; Fat: 6.66; Carb: 43.53; Protein: 3.59

Unreal Air Fryer Banana

Prep Time: 5 Mins   Cook Time: 20 Mins   Serves: 2

Ingredients:

- 2 medium bananas, peeled and sliced on a diagonal into 1/2" pieces
- 1 tablespoon coconut palm sugar
- 1/2 teaspoon cinnamon
- 1/2 teaspoon pure vanilla extract
- 1 teaspoon olive oil

Directions:

1. Slice bananas on a slight diagonal and add to a bowl, then sprinkle in the coconut sugar, cinnamon, and vanilla.
2. Gently stir and toss together so that the bananas are coated.
3. Lightly grease the bottom of the air fryer basket with olive oil to prevent sticking.
4. Evenly place the banana slices in the air fryer basket, making sure that none are overlapping.
5. Air fry at 350 degrees F for 10 minutes, flipping half way through.
6. Serve warm as desired! Enjoy!

Nutritional Value (Amount per Serving):

Calories: 145; Fat: 3.19; Carb: 30.03; Protein: 1.48

Air Fryer Honey Pecans

Prep Time: 5 Mins   Cook Time: 20 Mins   Serves: 6

Ingredients:

- 3 cups pecans
- ½ cup honey
- ½ teaspoon ground cinnamon

Directions:

1. In a large bowl, combine honey and pecans, then add the cinnamon and mix until well coated.
2. Place the nuts in the air fryer basket in a single layer.
3. Cook at 250 degrees F for 5-6 minutes. If not cooked enough, you can cook for an additional 1 to 2 minutes until the nuts are golden and the coating is bubbly. Keep a close eye on them so they don't burn.
4. Remove the nuts and spread them out on a lined baking tray to cool before serving.

Nutritional Value (Amount per Serving):

Calories: 428; Fat: 35.63; Carb: 30.31; Protein: 4.63

Air Fryer Apple Crisps

Prep Time: 5 Mins   Cook Time: 30 Mins   Serves: 2

Ingredients:

Filling Ingredients:
- 1 Apple, diced (I used pink lady)
- ½ tsp. Cinnamon
- ½ tbsp. Maple Syrup
- ½ tbsp. Lemon Juice

Topping Ingredients:
- ⅓ cup Old Fashioned / Rolled Oats
- 1 tbsp. Butter, melted
- 1 tbsp. Maple Syrup
- 1 tsp. Wholemeal / Whole Wheat Flour
- ½ tsp. Cinnamon

Directions:

1. Mix filling ingredients together, then divide evenly between two ramekins. Add one tablespoon of water to each ramekin on top of the filling ingredients.
2. Mix topping ingredients together, then divide evenly over the filling.
3. Cover with foil, then place in the air fryer basket and cook for 15 minutes on 350F.

Remove foil and continue to cook on 350°F for 5-10 minutes, until topping is crisp and golden and the filling is fork tender.

4. Serve warm as is, or with Greek yogurt, ice cream or whipped cream.

Nutritional Value (Amount per Serving):

Calories: 168; Fat: 5.17; Carb: 35.1; Protein: 3.39

Air Fryer Cinnamon Sugar Tortilla Chips

Prep Time: 2 Mins   Cook Time: 10 Mins   Serves: 4

Ingredients:

- ½ cup Granulated sugar
- 2 teaspoon Ground cinnamon
- 2 Tablespoon Butter, melted
- 4 Flour tortillas (8 inch)

Directions:

1. Add your sugar and cinnamon to a small bowl. Mix together until well combined.
2. Melt your butter in another bowl and brush it over the front and back of a flour tortilla.
3. Sprinkle cinnamon sugar over the butter. Rub the sugar mixture around the front and backside of the tortilla to coat it well.
4. Use a pizza cutter to slice the tortilla into wedges. Repeat with all tortillas.
5. Line your air fryer basket with some parchment paper and lay the cinnamon-coated tortillas in an even layer on the parchment.
6. Air fry for 6-8 minutes at 350 degrees F. Make sure to shake the basket halfway through.
7. After the chips are finished, remove them and place them on a wire rack or plate to cool before serving. Be careful as they will be hot.

Nutritional Value (Amount per Serving):

Calories: 225; Fat: 6.63; Carb: 37.57; Protein: 4.01

Air-Fryer Apple Slices

Prep Time: 5 Mins   Cook Time: 20 Mins   Serves: 4

Ingredients:

- 3 small apples, peeled and cut into 1/2-inch slices
- 1 tablespoon pure maple syrup
- 1 teaspoon grated orange zest
- 1 teaspoon canola oil
- 1 teaspoon vanilla extract
- ½ teaspoon ground cinnamon
- ⅛ teaspoon salt

Directions:

1. Preheat air fryer to 375°F for 5 minutes. Lightly coat the fryer basket with cooking spray.
2. Combine apple slices, maple syrup, orange zest, oil, vanilla, cinnamon and salt in a medium bowl; toss well to coat. Working in batches if necessary, spread the apple slices in a single layer in the fryer basket. Cook until the apples are tender and browned at the edges, about 12 minutes.

Nutritional Value (Amount per Serving):

Calories: 86; Fat: 1.32; Carb: 19.33; Protein: 0.31

Air Fryer Twice Baked Dessert Sweet Potatoes

Prep Time: 10 Mins   Cook Time: 18 Mins   Serves: 4

Ingredients:

- 2 cooked sweet potatoes
- 2 tablespoons butter, melted
- 2 tablespoons maple syrup
- 1/2 teaspoon cinnamon
- 1/4 teaspoon nutmeg
- 1/4 teaspoon salt, or to taste
- 2 tablespoons pecans, optional
- 1/4 cup mini marshmallows

Directions:

1. Start with 2 cooked sweet potatoes. It is easier to scoop out and stuff them if they are cold.
2. Slice each sweet potato in half. Scoop out the filling, leaving a 1/4 inch rim around the sides. Set the potato shells aside.
3. Mix the sweet potato insides with the melted butter, maple syrup, cinnamon, nutmeg and salt. Use a potato masher to mix it all together thoroughly.
4. Scoop the mixture back into the sweet potato shells, pressing it down into the shells.
5. Bake in the air fryer at 380 degrees F for 5 minutes.
6. Sprinkle the pecans, mini marshmallows or both on top of the sweet potatoes.

Bake in the air fryer at 380°F for 3 additional minutes.

Nutritional Value (Amount per Serving):

Calories: 164; Fat: 8.62; Carb: 21.53; Protein: 1.46

Air Fryer Banana Fritters

Prep Time: 10 Mins   Cook Time: 23 Mins   Serves: 4

Ingredients:

- Nonstick cooking spray
- 2 bananas
- 1/2 cup all-purpose flour
- 2 eggs, lightly beaten
- 1/2 cup unsweetened, shredded coconut
- 2 tablespoons sugar
- 1 teaspoon ground cinnamon
- Whipped cream or ice cream (optional for serving; for dairy-free diets, be sure to use a dairy-free version of either)

Directions:

1. Spray the bottom of your air fryer basket with the nonstick cooking spray and set aside.
2. Peel the bananas and cut them into 1-inch slices. Place the sliced bananas in a bowl and set aside.
3. Place the flour in a bowl and set aside.
4. Then, in a medium bowl, combine the coconut, cinnamon, and sugar. Stir to combine.
5. Working with one slice at a time, dip each slice into the bowl with the flour to coat it. Then, dip the banana slice into the egg to coat. Finally, coat each slice with the shredded coconut mixture.
6. Place the coated banana slices in the air fryer basket. Try to keep the banana slices in a single layer without touching each other.
7. Set the temperature to 375°F for 4 minutes. Then, use tongs to turn the banana slices over. Cook for another 3-4 minutes, or until the fritters have started to turn a golden brown on the outside.
8. Serve warm, plain or with your choice of whipped cream or ice cream.

Nutritional Value (Amount per Serving):

Calories: 363; Fat: 9.09; Carb: 66.7; Protein: 8.43

APPENDIX RECIPE INDEX

Made in United States
Troutdale, OR
02/13/2024

17663146R00062